You
&
I
Together

Copyright © 1996 by Daniel J. Shepard

All rights reserved. No part of this book may be reproduced in any form or by any electronic or mechanical means including information storage and retrieval systems without permission in writing from the publisher, except in case of reprints in the context of reviews.

Library of Congress Catalog Number: 96–67578 (paper)
                                      96–68766 (hardcover)

Publisher's Cataloging in Publication
(Prepared by Quality Books Inc.)

Shepard, Daniel J.
    You & I Together / by Daniel J. Shepard.
    p.cm.
    LCCN: 96-67578/96-68766
    ISBN: 1-882792-23-8 (paper)
    ISBN: 1-882792-24-6 (hardcover)

    1. Philosophy   I. Title.   II. Title: You and I together.
B945.S44S44 1996   191
                                        QBI96-20335

Proctor Publications
P.O. Box 2498
Ann Arbor, Michigan 48106
(313) 480-9900

To order, please contact:
W. E. Hope, Inc.
118 Main Center, Suite 226
Northville, Michigan 48167
(810) 349-1317

Illustrations provided by Gary Book

Printed in the United States of America

You
&
I
Together

by
Daniel J. Shepard

Proctor Publications, L.L.C., Ann Arbor, Michigan

Dedicated To:

My Children With Love:

Christopher
Danielle
Scott

and with Love to
My Wife and Friend:

Nancy

Inspiration To Initiate The Writing Of This Book

Provided by:

Steven Hawking

*A man I have never met
But for whom I have
The utmost respect and admiration.
A man who has provided many
The courage to go on.*

TABLE OF CONTENTS

FROM THE AUTHOR TO THE READER
From One Soul to Another, From the Heart..................1

FORMAT
An Essential Element of the Book....................7

PREFACE
Man, Religion, the Soul, and the Stars are not Incompatible; They are a Symbiotic Necessity....................11

BOOK I: "the philosophy"..........................16

Introduction
A Purpose is the Purpose of a Philosophy..................19

1. **God**..................23
2. **Quadratic vs. Linear Philosophy**
   Noncontradicting Contradictions.............33
3. **B.E.G.A. Begins**
   Bernoulli, Einstein, Grandi, Asimov Lead us Here....................41
4. **Sets of 4 Parallel Universes**
   From Bernoulli to Grandi with a Twist of Asimov....................53
5. **The Universe**
   One of Many Laboratories for Creative Thought....................61
6. **Universes**
   Limitless Limits....................69

7. **The "Ripple Effect"**
   Hedonism, Religion, Responsibilities......77
8. **The Mechanism**
   What Happens when the Universe Implodes..89
9. **The Missing Link**
   Evolution isn't the Only Subject with a Missing Link..97
10. **Omnipotence/Omnipresence/ Omniscience**
    Man Playing God........................107

11. **In Summary**
    Simply Put................................117

BOOK II: *The Impact*

A. MAN
The Individual/The Species......128

Introduction
Man A Machine?......131

12. **Man's Inhumanity to Man**
    Does no one Remember? Will Someone Please Make it Stop?......139
13. **Man's Good Side**
    We are our Brother's Keeper......147
14. **Is it Worth it in the End?**
    Is there Really a Heaven and a Hell?......161
15. **Is There Hope for You as an Individual?**
    Hope is all we Have......169
16. **Is There Hope for Mankind?**
    The Swirling Waters of the Lack of Conviction Continue Eroding Away the Pillars......179
17. **Religion**
    Is it Really Significant /Necessary?......189

18. **In Summary**
    The Soul......199

B. MAN'S SOCIETY/THE PRESENT
Social Dilemmas are not Dilemmas..........................206

Introduction
The Crumbling Foundation...209

19. Status
Social/Occupational/Economic Illusions, Perpetuated by the Ones it Hurts Most....221

20. Atheism/Religion
The Atheist has a Soul, He too is God, But yet a Lonely Place He Occupies..............231

21. War/Abortion
Take Care of your own Soul....................239

22. Suicide
So you don't Feel so Good?......................251

23. Death Penalty/Life Incarceration
A "Debt to Society" is a Debt Owed to Other Souls, It Can Never be Repaid................259

24. Letting Go/Forgiving
You do not Need to Punish Men – They will Bring on their Own Punishment – Move on With Your Life......................................271

25. Missionary Work/Helping Others
Everybody is a Missionary, Like it or Not..281

26. In Summary
Intolerance is an Outmoded Term..........293

C. MAN
Historical Reflections and the Future......302

Introduction
Predestination/Free Will, Both at the Same Time.....305

27. God/gods
A Name Does Not Make God.................315
28. Good/Bad
No such Thing as Good and Bad...........327
29. Heaven/Hell
Some Things are Worth Repeating..........333
30. God is Going to Get You for That
God has no need to Inflict Vengeance Upon Himself..................341
31. Christianity/Religions
All are One..............................351
32. Jesus Christ/"the Philosophy"
There is no Conflict.................361

33. In Summary
History is Meant to Guide One into the Future...................367

THE BOOK IN SUMMARY
Two Statements/Nine Words.................377

A Special Page of Thanks................380
Addendum: To My Students.................381
Suggested Reading List...................386
About the Author.........................387

> *"Me, you – we're no more than travelers."*
> Mohammed Dib (b. 1920)
> Algerian writer

FROM THE AUTHOR TO THE READER
♦
From one soul to another, from the heart

This book cannot be all things to all people. It cannot be a scholarly study with footnotes, formal research, cross references, and bibliography while at the same time discuss all the issues that need addressing by man, that need addressing by what the book intends to initiate: a universal, comprehensive philosophy of the soul, of life.

As one reads the book, much will be going on in one's mind, many questions regarding the philosophy will be raised. Many shortcomings regarding the lack of writing research and techniques will surface. Much denial will take place regarding topics and concepts presented in order to attempt to keep intact one's own convictions and spiritual beliefs. Some sections will hold no interest for some because they are not at that point in their life. Some sections will interest others because they *are* at that point in their lives.

All of this is as it should be, as it is meant to be, in the writing of this book. Pardon my digression from the importance of "the philosophy" but this is one arena I am going to use to explain, or make excuses for, the reasoning of the format of the book.

A. The writing research:

I am not a scholar, an intellectual, or a renown philosopher. The formal research, the bibliographies, the cross references are going to have to wait for someone far more scholarly than I. The research is going to have to come over a greater span of time than I have to give in this reality. My short fifty years of reflection and readings have come through a somewhat primitive educational background, semi-isolation from society, and a totally bewildered understanding of why men constantly reject each other when all of us have so many shortcomings in spite of all the religious background we've been exposed to.

To put it more simply, this book needs to be written, this concept needs a jump start and my life is too short to do it in a manner everyone thinks they would have done it or would have liked it to be done. In addition, the book is already too voluminous, and others may want to follow it up with more scientific validity. There is much left to be done.

B. Techniques:

The book orients around short topics. This is done to reduce the mundane and monotonous droning of introspection by the author. It is done to begin to get one to reflect and then leave one intentionally hanging in order to encourage one to start thinking.

The book includes graphics, illustrations, quotations, and pictures to help readers of all levels to begin to understand the overall direction of the book and to perk the reader's interest.

The summaries briefly outline what was addressed. If portions of it seem enticing or intriguing, that is just what it is meant to do. Many interesting philosophical ideas get lost in verbalization and ink. Whether this is successful or not will be up to you to decide.

C. Reader denial related to topics and concepts presented:

Readers, in order to attempt to keep their own convictions and spiritual beliefs totally intact, will want to reject the parts that do not reinforce their personal beliefs; but what good is that? If the rejection is done in the realm of rejection through logic and reflection, then the book has been a success.

The purpose of the book, after all, is to get one to think, to reflect, to find solutions to our present and future problems through a rational development of a cohesive, unifying understanding of life's purpose in this reality.
My belief is that this will come only through the development of a rational, logical, comprehensive, all-encompassing philosophy of life and our purpose as men within this reality.

D. Reader acceptance related to topics and concepts presented:

Nice, but if the whole book were nothing but a reiteration of one's beliefs, it would not need to be written. Therefore, one should not just read the sections with which one agrees.

The purpose is to get one to think. The purpose is to get someone to think. Maybe, if it is successful, it will get many people to think and one of those people may be able to put the concept in a more acceptable manner to others. Maybe that in turn will spark others to follow suit in their own manner, and a snowball effect will follow.

E. Some sections having no interest for the reader:

People are at different points in their lives. People have different interests. That is as it should be and the sections in part II, "The Impact", which have no interest to you should be just scanned or skipped. The more one reads of the total picture, however, the more one will begin to understand the true nature and purpose of "the philosophy" and your own purpose within the reality of our universe.

F. Sections of interest but frustrating in their brevity:

These will be areas of interest because the reader may be at that point of their journey in life. To these people, I apologize. I do not have the background nor the space to write the type of book you want or need.

If this book, however, sparks an interest, if this book encourages you to seek out other sources, it will have been partially successful.

G. Genderizing the writing and political correctness:

I strongly considered genderizing the terminology of man and men into a more politically correct format of man, woman, men, women, humankind, boys, girls, male, female, children, peoplekind, and on and on.

But this book is not about the battle of the sexes. It is not about man's body. It is about the very essence of each and every life form in this universe. It is about the very essence of each and every life form in all realities. This book is about the soul itself. This book is not about the machines the souls occupy, but about who we are as fellow souls, each making its own personal journey through its own personal reality. It is about travelling together not as machines with maleness, femaleness, presexual maturity, colorations of skin; rather it is a book about our very essence travelling together with the very essence of others.

It is not about sexual orientation, intelligence, beauty, brains, and brawn. This book rises above the struggles of man and men to the level of the soul itself, the essence of all intelligent life. This book is a step above the petty power struggles of mankind. It leaves the pettiness of our present world behind in order to make sense of who we are as men and what our actual purpose is in this reality so that we may then reexamine just what the function is of the machines we occupy, regardless of that very machine's internal as well as external characteristics.

With this established, it is my hope, that "men" can then return to the reality of our present awareness with a new respect for each other. Return with a better understanding of our purpose in reality which will lead us eventually to recognize the phenomenal waste of energy we are expending upon petty, nonsensical, counterproductive, irrelevant power struggles.

Hopefully we as humankind, all people, will have a new awareness of who we really are and will find tolerance and acceptance to be a new foundation for our new millennium. It is time we see each other as souls, as brothers, as one, not as machines with different exteriors and interiors.

For those of you reading this book, I say go out, seek what you need, do what you feel your soul compels you to accomplish. If you cannot find your answers, remember you are not the only one seeking answers. Answers do not come easily. Maybe this is where your quest leads you in life. Take heart. The journey through life takes many turns. Pick yourself up, and begin your quest. It may be in total isolation from others. It may be in partial isolation, as was mine. It may be in a group setting, as is the journey of many. It may be a combination of all three.

My quest seems to have been one of developing answers to mans' age old questions:
> What is man?
> Why are we here?
> What is our purpose in this reality?
> What is my purpose in this reality?
> **So. . .what's the point of it all?**

"The noblest in quality and highest in rank of all human activities is philosophy... The philosopher's aim in his theoretical studies is to ascertain the truth; in his practical knowledge, to conduct himself in accordance with that truth."

Rasa'il al-Kindi (810 – 873)
Arab philosopher and physician

FORMAT
♦
An Essential Element of the Book

This book has been written with built-in features as well as a sequential progression. The total picture of "the philosophy" cannot be grasped with understanding, unless the book is read in sequence, just as a person's life cannot be understood looking at isolated incidences in that life.

The quotations have two purposes:

> One: they are intended to provide an awareness that although some of the ideas are my own, the total work is a coalescence of thinkers who have permeated the history of mankind.

> Two: they are intended to help validify, simplify, and clarify the concepts addressed.

The commas are, for the most part, not a grammatical tool, but rather a literary tool used to cause one to literally pause when reading, in order to grasp a thought within a thought.

The terms, "man", "men", "mankind", etc., are intended to be genderless. These terms are used in the universal sense of the soul, our very essence.

The **bolded** terms are terms which have been or will be discussed in detail later in the book.

Each topic in the book is followed with a brief summary which is intended to give an overview of concepts and insights that have been touched upon in the chapter.

The sequence of the book is:

Preface:	Establishment of a reason for a general philosophy.
Introduction:	Establishment of why the book was written in the first place.
Part I:	Establishment of what the general philosophy is.
Part II:	Applying the philosophy, since philosophies have little meaning if they cannot be functional.
Part A:	Applying the philosophy to man as an individual; applying the philosophy to man as a species.
Part B:	Applying the philosophy to society today.
Part C:	Applying the philosophy to many of mans' historical reflections in order to rethink the future.

This book is not intended to be "the way" or "right". It is intended to cause one to pause in the midst of the chaotic, demanding, and incessant pace of life, and to reflect upon oneself as an individual and as a significant unit within society. It is intended to cause one to reflect upon oneself, to reflect upon how we each effect others in society, and how we each effect society as a whole. What one is doing, where one is headed, and how one interacts within society will have an effect upon one's awareness, as an entity, for eternity, through the **"ripple effect"**.

It is a book intended to open your eyes, and cause you to realize that there are many exciting ideas all around us. These ideas are just waiting for someone to reflect upon them and express them from a slightly different point of view.

This is not a book to be read all at once, or in a rapidly scanned fashion. It is intended to be read slowly, over time, in pieces, and reread again for a deeper understanding as to the significance of what it is implying. The pieces read, are intended to be mulled over in one's head, and mixed with one's convictions, in order to cause the reader to come to terms with their own beliefs, and who they are as an individual.

10   *You & I Together*

"I believe with perfect faith that the Creator, blessed be his name, is not a body, and that he is free from all accidents of matter, and that he has not any form whatsoever."

Malmonides (1135 – 1204)
Spanish Hebrew Philosopher
Thirteen Principles

PREFACE
♦
Man, Religion, the Soul, and the Stars are not Incompatible; They Are a Symbiotic Necessity

For: Chris, Danni, and Scott

I am a Christian but my writings are about the universality of God, man's and mans' tie to God, man's and mans' purpose in life, all religions, not just Christianity, and their importance and lack of importance to man's eternal life. It is about eternal life itself and the reality of that idea. It is about heaven and hell, and why all Christians are heading to both just as are all men of all faiths.

It is a flow of words generated from the heart as well as the mind. It's a culmination of philosophical ideas intended to broaden your mind and expand your tolerance. It's a book dealing with today and a book dealing with tomorrow. Go out into the world, learn from the past, but do not linger in it. Live in the present, but control it – do not let it control you. Look to the future, but not in fear – rather in excitement for the new challenges to come.

Read, read, read. There are many novel, exciting, and mind-expanding ideas out there for you to discover. Read *The Celestine Prophecy* and *Mutant Message Downunder*. Each touched upon the special place Man has in this universe and a purpose Man has in this eternity. I did not find a completeness with these works, but I did sense that these authors also were possibly touched by Mans' purpose in the scheme of eternity, whether they realized it in their hearts or not. Obviously, as a Christian, other books have given me a sense of God and a sense of mans' purpose in the picture of eternity. These books include not only the Bible, but authors such as C.S. Lewis, and Norman Vincent Peale. All these works have left me with more of a sense of abrupt termination. They never reached the point of explaining mans' purpose in life or how or where we, as pieces of the jigsaw puzzle of "life", fit into that puzzle. Nor did they explain how or where each of us as individuals fit into this puzzle. Even the Bible had its problems with symbolism, insinuation, and lost historical meaning created by a multiplicity of sometimes good-intentioned, and sometimes not good-intentioned, men. Their attempts, over a relatively long span of time, at translating a valuable training manual to fit their own historical cultural beliefs proved to create understandable inaccuracies and misconceptions, just as had interpretations of other like historical documents.

As I read books, it seemed they all missed the big picture. They all directed themselves into the mode of perpetuating their own beliefs on a shallow level and lost track of mans' reaching for the stars. They seemed to be helping stigmatize man to a terrestrial life form when in fact we are intended for the heavens. Before man can leap to the stars, he must come to terms with himself, his fellow men, and himself as a species. He must see his purpose in life and his place in this universe, and be comfortable with both. Man must see how his "Journey to the Moon" fits in with E.T.'s visit and how they are both compatible with himself, God, Allah, Christ, and the karma of all men.

We cannot come to terms with ourselves, however, until we answer the puzzle in life regarding our purpose as individuals and as a species. Once we have solved this puzzle, we will have freed our energies up for the beautiful and exciting journey to the stars and we will have brought not only ourselves to peace internally, but given rise to the opportunity for all men to feel the same. We will finally have reached our first universal purpose as physical terrestrial life forms, which will, in turn, allow us to leap from this beautiful blue and white sphere into the immensity of space.

In addition, we will also have reached the understanding that our true essence lies not in our physical self, but in our conscious self or soul. We will have come to peace with all our fellow men and we will have finally come to peace with the concept all religions teach, which is that we are all truly brothers. We all need each other no matter how different we may appear. We all, each and every one, have a niche to fill in life. I hope this book will shed light upon this fact, act as one more step in our attempt to fulfill our purpose on this earthly planet, and help lead us to our next step as a species, which is a leap to the stars.

We cannot and will not be able to make the leap significantly until we have come to terms with ourselves, accept our fellow man as our fellow man, regardless of color or religion, and be able to feel free to act as unique individuals within the framework of a cohesive unified species.

We have all the pieces of the puzzle to do this. When we look around ourselves, the world seems to be tearing itself apart:

crime, famine, global inhumanity of man to man, disease, pestilence, and especially the intolerance of individuals to individuals. How can this be a good time? How can this be a threshold of our greatest leap to understanding ourselves, reaching for the stars, and touching God? It does not seem to make sense. It seems to be contradictory in nature, but it isn't. Human-generated chaos and catastrophes exist because we are at the dawning of a new age for mankind. We are so anxious to make the quantum leap that we are overextending all aspects of our societies and we are not coordinating our overall energies to unify the efforts we have already established. We are lacking a simple universal philosophy that embraces all people, cultures, religions, and traditions. We are lacking a universal philosophy that will unite people rather than splinter them. We are lacking the understanding of our purpose as individuals and as a species.

A simple example of this is welfare in its present form. It is well-intentioned in its attempt to aid our fellow man, but it is, in fact, destructive in its present falsely compassionate form, since it destroys the sense of self-worth within the individual. It was not developed maliciously but rather in a vacuum. It was developed with no universal philosophy of either the purpose or understanding of man or mankind to guide its path; rather it just drifted into its present form.

We have all the pieces to make the leap to peace and unity of man and man to himself, but in our excitement, we are not letting our left hand help our right. It's like building a tower of blocks and we are 999 pieces high and need to place our last piece. Using both hands will allow one hand to stabilize the other and allow the task to be completed successfully. We must take a breath, unite our hands, and finish the task.

"What a chimera then is man! What a novelty! What a monster, what a chaos, what a contradiction, what a prodigy! Judge of all things, feeble earthworm, depository of truth, a sink of uncertainty and error, the glory and the shame of the universe."

Blaise Pascal
(1623 – 1662)

"The accumulated experience of history teaches us that, when no one looks after people, the people take care of themselves; and when the people take care of themselves, it is no river that runs along in its riverbed, but a deluge that inundates."

Rafael Enriquez de Zayas
(1848 – 1932)
Mexican Writer, Porfirio Diaz
la evolucion de se vidao

Book I:

♦

"the philosophy"

♦

You & I Together

BOOK I: "the philosophy" 16
Introduction
A Purpose is the Purpose of a Philosophy...............19

1. God............23
2. Quadratic vs. Linear Philosophy
   Noncontradicting Contradictions............33
3. B.E.G.A. Begins
   Bernoulli, Einstein, Grandi, Asimov Lead us Here............41
4. Sets of 4 Parallel Universes
   From Bernoulli to Grandi with a Twist of Asimov............53
5. The Universe
   One of Many Laboratories for Creative Thought............61
6. Universes
   Limitless Limits............69
7. The "Ripple Effect"
   Hedonism, Religion, Responsibilities......77
8. The Mechanism
   What Happens when the Universe Implodes............89
9. The Missing Link
   Evolution isn't the Only Subject with a Missing Link............97
10. Omnipotence/Omnipresence/Omniscience
    Man Playing God............107

11. In Summary
    Simply Put............117

18   You & I Together

Climb high
Climb far
Your goal the sky
Your aim the star.

Inscription on Hopkins Memorial Steps,
William's College
Williamstown, Massachusetts

INTRODUCTION
♦
A Purpose, is the Purpose, of a Philosophy

"The purpose" of a total philosophy, is to completely address all issues of "life". The purpose of this book is to outline a total philosophy of life. Not life in the sense of mortal life, but rather in the all encompassing sense of, "life" before "life", followed by "life", followed by "life" after "life". A beginning and end to a circle with no beginning or end.

It attempts to extract from what we already know, but find fragmented, and build a simple universal philosophy of man and mankind. It attempts to identify the purpose of such seemingly inconsequential beings as man, men, and mankind within the historically assumed infinite expanse of the universe.

It is a book intent on not destroying, but building. It is a book intent on accelerating intolerance to intolerance. It is a book intent on initiating contemplation and meditation upon man's and mans' inhumanity to man, whether it be in a small individualistic behavior, an isolated small social way, or a repugnant large scale social form.

It is a description of a philosophy that reinforces and maintains the importance of our past history, cultures, and traditions. It is a philosophy that accounts for mans' past deja vu and "gut" feelings.

It is a philosophy that manages to provide a process of solving today's social and individualistic dilemmas, yet allows for an open-minded approach to tomorrow's problems. It is a book with a philosophy intended to unify, not splinter, the individual, people, social and religious groups, and men as men.

It as·an attempt at using the past, agonizing with the present, and reflecting upon the future in order to build a working philosophy that will allow all men to feel a commonality with each other as brothers, not just in this life, but from their past lives and into their future lives.

Will this book be successful at accomplishing all these grandiose goals? Success is not the point here. The point, rather, is the direction this book takes, not whether it gets us there. Much greater thinkers than I will someday reach these goals if they develop a total philosophy encompassing all aspects of man and men rather than use philosophy as a tool to reflect upon fragmented ideas.

"In Summary"

Understanding Precedes Solutions

A Sample Of A Universal Philosophy

Joining Fragmented Pieces

Principle #1: Build Upon What You Already Have

Principle #2: Respect Your Traditions, Cultures, History

Principle #3: Build Functional Models

Principle #4: Unification Is The Key

Success Is Not The Point Here

God

24 You & I Together

Some fools declare that God created the universe. If God created the universe, where was He before creation? Did God create the universe out of something? If He did, who created the material out of which He created the universe? ...

Mahapurana (c. 9th century)
Jain sacred text

Chapter 1
♦
God

God and man: unusual concepts that have gone hand in hand since the recorded history of man, regardless of the time in history, or the culture recording the history. Why? Good question and a rather insightful and perhaps directional one at that. It is beginning to appear that the more universally generated a concept is among men, the more truth one will find as one shucks away the myths, culture, and tradition which has blossomed around it.

Man has always believed in God. Some say from hope, others say from fear. Some say from intelligence, others say from ignorance. Some say from tradition and others say from faith. Whatever one professes, men have always oriented their philosophical discussions around God or god.

Even those professing to not believe in a God, have professed their true hidden beliefs and doubts through the very fact that they argue against God, for if there is no God, why even bother arguing about the concept of God? If there is truly no God, there is no significance in the end anyway, thus there is no point in arguing the issue. Could it be then, that those arguing the point in a negative fashion are merely seeking proof that they are wrong?

But back to the term God. Just what is God? Is He what the Christians conceptualize is God, "The true and only God"? Is the Great Spirit in the heavens the true God? Perhaps Allah is the true God. Perhaps Zeus is the true God and the other ancient Greek Gods are in a sense as the Christian Angels. Or perhaps they are all one in the same. Perhaps the error in Christian, or for that matter most religious thought, is that God is not a particular God but everyone's God. Perhaps we are more brothers in the soul and in beliefs than we as any particular culture care to think.

Whatever one's belief, the fact remains that man has, to our knowledge, always conceptualized God, or a form of God in some sense, and therefore perhaps this small seed, this nugget of universality of man, is true.

Some say wait a minute. Not so fast. If there is a God, and God is God, and if by definition God is the creator of our reality, then who created God's reality? If God is the **omnipotent**, then who had the omnipotence to create God the Omnipotent? If all things have a beginning, and God is the Beginning of all things, then who began the beginning of God, and wouldn't that force in fact be God? A perplexing problem, but perhaps not as perplexing as one might think.

The answer is simply, no, for by definition our God is the initiation of mans' reality. The force that created the reality of mankind is our God. Simple? Yes, simple.

Then one might say this does not truly explain who the God of

God, the creator of God's reality, and the God of that God is, etc. That is true. Then one might say, well I want to know who God is. In other words, one might say I want to know who the God of God is and the God of that God. That is unfortunate. You are jumping ahead of yourself, or should I say you are jumping ahead of mans' position in our space time continuum. For as one cannot understand the subatomic particles until one understands the concept of an atom, and as one cannot understand the function of a mitochondria until one understands the concept of a cell, one cannot understand God's God until one understands his own God. Thus, until we, as a relatively intelligent and philosophical species, have a better grasp of our own creator, we are just going to have to wait for any significant insight into the picture greater than God. Man is not a patient animal, but sometimes he has no option but to wait.

Does this mean we are to stop our search for our true spiritual Creator? By no means! We have always and will always need to search, if for no other reason than it is an intuitive part of our nature. In order to obtain the beginnings or a better realization of who God's God is, we must first obtain a better understanding of who our God is.

Does this mean we should stop believing in our God? Quite the contrary, for our beliefs, our traditions, our heritage in religious customs give us peace, tranquillity, security, roots, guidance, civility, and a rock upon which we may weather our doubts until we, in time, come to understand the true and focused picture of God. In the meantime don't despair, for at some point we will obtain a better picture of God. Keep in mind that God is God and will remain so regardless of what we do or what we wish to believe, or regardless of how we wish to paint Him.

Each of us must search for the customs and personal beliefs that comfort us best as particular individuals. Each of us must recognize that we all are searching, and be tolerant of each other's search and help each other find our own particular niche in our own particular times. We must revolutionize our religions to allow for each man's search and tolerance for a particular religion that suits his or her own particular, unique needs and biological energy patterns. Religions must become tolerant towards each other, stop believing as if they are the only truth and light, and begin realizing that they are only one of many. Religions each have a crucial part to play in mans' and man's overall purpose. They are meant to be unique, not because that makes one right and one wrong, but because that provides for the needed variation to allow for the diversity of so many. The variations in religions thus provide a niche in religious customs that will allow each of us to find inner peace.

As we gain more knowledge as a species and as individuals, we become even more individualistic as an entity in the sea of humanity. This leads to even greater needs for variety and what appears to be major variations in religion, but in actuality proves to be, in regards to the immensely large picture, relatively minor differences in customs and beliefs. This then, in turn, accommodates the need for more niches created through the acquisition of more knowledge by man. And so the cycle goes. This need for a means of filling unique religious niches leads to a need to assist each other (**missionary work**) in finding these niches in order to help each other as brothers find peace and tranquillity.

This revolutionary reversal of the religious frame of mind regarding the concept of "I'm right and you are wrong", however, cannot begin until we as individuals insist upon it within our religious groups in large enough numbers. And this cannot begin until we are willing to accept that God is God and not who we dress Him up to be. We cannot create God; God has created us. We cannot insist that God is who we have, through time and custom, drawn Him to be, but rather we must understand that who we have drawn Him to be through time and custom was who we needed Him to be in order to find our niche. He is who He is to ourselves, because we needed Him to be such in order to find comfort in our lack of knowledge and to assuage our fears of what we perceive to be mortality.

We must recognize this process of painting a security picture of God before we can truly begin to show tolerance and empathy for our fellow man's painting of God. Once we have truly accepted this concept, we will begin to accept our fellow man as our true brothers in soul. Regardless of when this metamorphism to tolerance within society occurs, and it will occur, God will remain who He is – God – and not who we wish to paint Him as. There is nothing, no matter how hard we try, that we will be able to do about it.

This, then, leads us to Circular Philosophies – Quadratics vs. Linear.

God

"In Summary"

The Search

God Belongs To Everyone

Man And man Are Different Concepts With Two Different Purposes

It Is Time For People Of ALL Religions To Revolt Against Religion

Key Concept: Tolerance And Empathy

Religion Is What Comforts The Soul

You & I Together

"the philosophy" 33

Chapter 2: Quadratic vs. Linear Philosophies

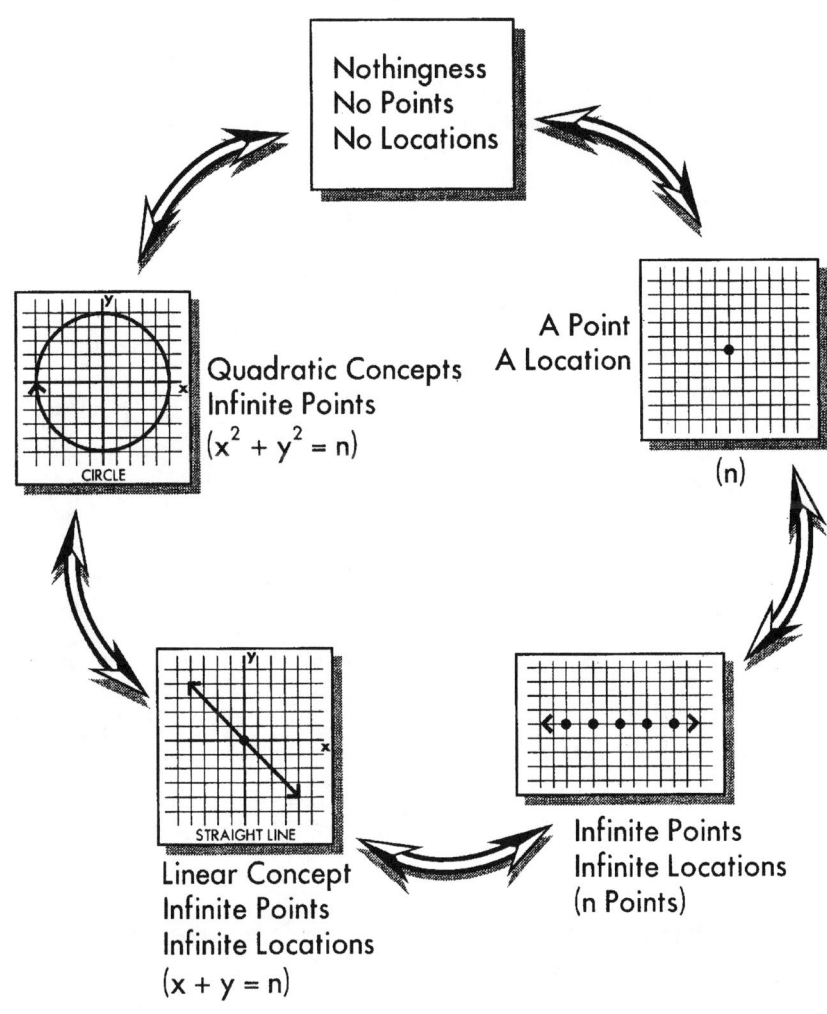

*The south has a limit and no limit,
The sun is declining when it is at high noon,
A creature is dying when it is born.*
                             Hur Shi (c. 370 – 290 B.C.E.)
                                          Chinese philosopher

Quadratic vs. Linear Philosophies
♦
Noncontradictory Contradictions

Mankind has always been faced with perplexing contradictions. Man has always been stymied by an endless array of contradictions from the earliest of recorded times to the present. These same contradictions have haunted man probably since the beginning of mans' earliest history. The strange thing is, that as long as we have been obsessed with these constantly recurring concepts that seem to haunt the souls of all men, and as long as we have been trying to excise them from our souls through religion and scientific dissection, we have never been able to rid our subconscious minds of these annoying thoughts and premonitions that seem to dwell in our subconscious. They just bubble to the surface of our conscious self in a seemingly never-ending procession.

If water represented man's mind and awareness was mans' thoughts, emotions, insights, and knowledge, an analogy of this perplexing flow of recurrent universal, seemingly unprovable, contradictory yet noncontradictory ideas might easily go as follows:

Water from an underground spring bubbles to the surface from a mysterious source we cannot visually identify. The water from this spring is man's as well as mans' deja vu from his true beginnings into which he shall be absorbed again. This water in turn feeds a brook, which feeds a stream, which feeds a river, which feeds into an ocean. The ocean is all of mans' pool of conscious action, thoughts, and awareness. The ocean, river, stream, and brook are never able to expunge themselves of this spring water. However, the further these entities get from the source of the spring, the more perplexing the source of the water becomes. The further one gets from the source, the more difficult it is to recognize the pattern the pieces form, since the pieces are too jumbled and the distance between them too great to put them together in a comprehensive, conscious, visible picture.

Just what persistent haunting of the soul is man constantly being exposed to? People have free will, but they are responsible for their actions. Things don't just happen; they are meant to be. Man has a purpose, but we cannot reach a consensus on the universality of that purpose as a species. There is death, but it is the beginning of life. Man was created in the image of God, but how can God have such a limited form? All men are capable of good, but not all men are good. "Bad" things happen to "good" people. Hedonism, you are your brother's keeper, religion, predestination, morality, immorality, love, hate, joy, sorrow. The contradictions and attempts to resolve them have gone on forever and ever it seems. Perhaps the contradictions are not contradictions at all. Perhaps we have just been thinking about the logic of them in too simplistic a manner, yet not simplistic enough. Another contradiction? Maybe not, perhaps our philosophical thinking needs to jump into another mode.

In the past, we have always thought in terms of isolated concepts and straight line thought, or what one might term in mathematics as "linear" thoughts. Equations to the first power only. Examples of linear philosophy would be: the universe is limitless and goes infinitely far in any "one" direction. Life "begins" and life "ends" or others might say you go to eternal life. A "beginning" and an "end". Light travels in a "straight line"; the universe goes on forever.

Perhaps it is time to put our thoughts into another mode. Perhaps we need to think "quadratically". Perhaps we need to think in a curve. For example circles, represented by quadratic equations, have no beginning or end. Perhaps life has no beginning or end, just different places on a curved line composed of an infinite number of life experiences in different forms. Perhaps philosophy needs to think in terms of curves and circles rather than straight lines, quadratically instead of linearly. Nature, after all, is not composed of basically straight lines, so perhaps mans', or for that matter man's life experiences and purpose, would be better understood if we contemplated it in a quadratic format rather than a linear one, as we have historically done. Perhaps we need to think philosophically more in terms of circular thoughts or what one might call higher order equations.

At the same time, we might just need to take concepts of individual premonitions, science, philosophy, religion, and stop isolating them into uniquely different topics. Perhaps we need to expand meshing them together into a comprehensive picture.

One person contemplates the purpose of life, another analyzes the DNA structure. One person meditates upon the significance of man's actions upon his eternal soul, another develops a code of medical morality. One man considers the source of man's origin, another digs for the missing link. And one man reflects upon reincarnation, another investigates the definition of when life begins and ends.

Perhaps, in addition to thinking quadratically, we need to also apply matrix analysis to our thinking and begin to coordinate the merging of our thoughts into a universal picture. Perhaps we now have the information we need to get a basic picture of man's and mans' place in the universe. With the right philosophy, we can finally, truly, reach for the stars.

With the development of the concept of quadratics philosophy versus linear philosophy in mind, part II of this book will attempt to put forward an example of quadratic philosophical thinking merged with a matrix format to tie together "the philosophy" into a quasi-logical model that can answer many of mans' age old questions.

With this in mind, we can begin to examine many of mans' discoveries. We can begin to put isolated pieces of the jigsaw puzzle together and begin to view the total picture in the next section "B.E.G.A.", a section named after four great thinkers, Bernoulli, Einstein, Grandi, and Asimov.

Quadratic vs. Linear Philosophy
Noncontradicting Contradictions

"In Summary"

Linear Math Describes Straight Lines
One Dimensional
Linear Philosophies Describe Life In A
Beginning - End Format
One Dimensional Conceptualization

Quadratic Math Describes Circles
Two Dimensional
Quadratic Philosophies Describe Life In A
Circular Format
Two Dimensional Conceptualization

Just As On A Circle:

Universal Concepts Start From Somewhere
Circles Do Get You Somewhere
Going Back To The Beginning Is Man's Purpose
Deja Vu Is Not A Random Phenomenon
Life Has No Beginning Or End

40   *You & I Together*

Chapter 3: B.E.G.A. Begins

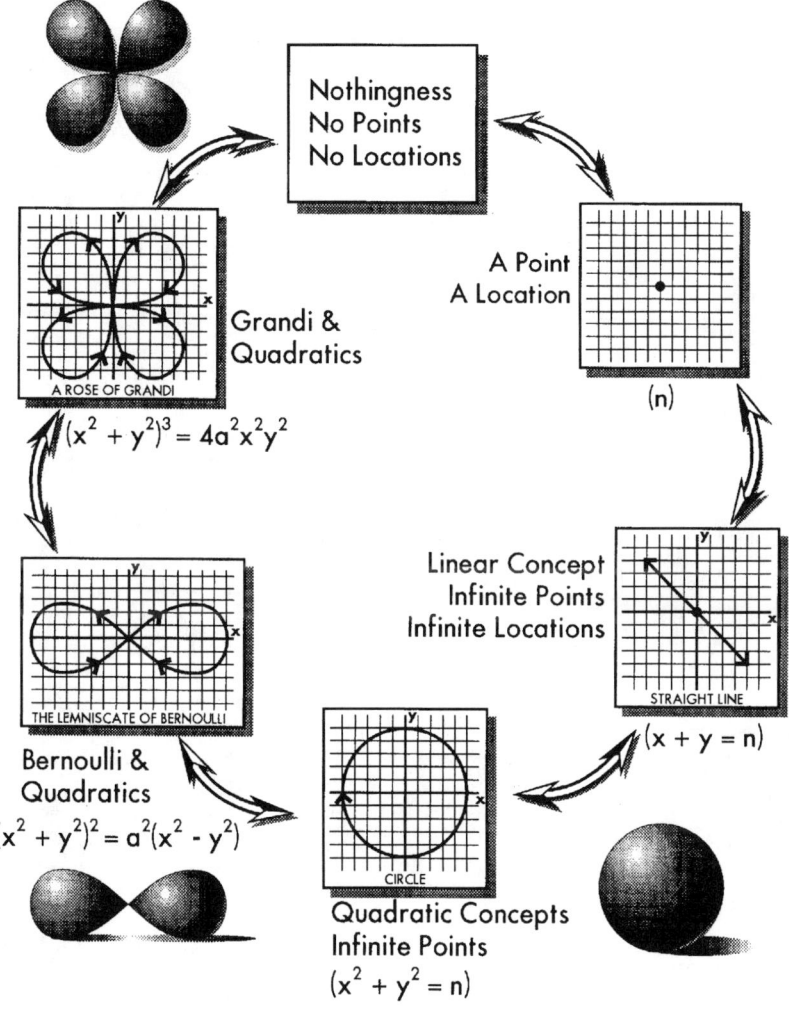

42 *You & I Together*

Great understanding is broad and unhurried; little understanding is cramped and busy.
Attributed to Buddha
(c. 563 – 483 B.C.E.)

B.E.G.A. Begins
♦
Bernoulli, Einstein, Grandi, Asimov Lead Us Here

Pieces of a puzzle held by many, put together, make a complete thought; kept they apart spark wonder, interest, uncertainty, but also the inability to move on.

One cannot move to the next major puzzle for mankind until one solves the first. One cannot even begin to understand what the next major puzzle for mankind will be since we are passing through what we perceive to be a one-dimensional time frame. Until man solves the puzzle blocking the journey of his soul through time, he will not comprehend the next puzzle he must face.

What greater puzzle of man's than the purpose of life, the purpose of the soul, your very purpose in life? What greater puzzle than to solve the age old question of why face life's trials, tribulations, joys, and happiness day after day?

Man began putting the puzzle together when he asked his first question, "Why?" Philosophers continued the task when they asked, "Why?" Religion assembled what they thought was the total puzzle when they said, "Because." Mathematicians assembled another portion of the puzzle, when they said, "Look!" Scientists and seekers of knowledge assembled still another portion when they found symmetry. Now all portions of the puzzle just need to be assembled to view the larger picture.

What happens when you put them all together? A bigger, more complete picture emerges. A complete universal philosophy, for this point in time, will emerge that is capable of initiating a realization of just why man can allow himself to be tolerant of all men. A realization of just why all men must accept each other as brothers. A realization of why and where we have gone wrong and where we have gone right in our thinking regarding man, men, and tolerance. Where do the mathematicians and scientists fit in with the age old questions of man and philosophers? Where do the mathematicians and scientists fit in with the religious doctrines developed over the millennia?

One needs to begin with the mathematician Bernoulli and conclude with the scientist Asimov and then fuse them into religion, philosophy, and mans' deja vu to put the puzzle together. So let's examine the process of the development of man and put some of the puzzle together and see where it leads. Let's begin to think in circles by beginning to think in terms of a point, a location in space. A circle so small it actually has no size at all. A circle because each location on the circle needs to be the same distance from the center so small it has no size itself. When reading the following, do not worry about understanding the formulas; they are there just to give the concept some validity. Just roll over them as you read and absorb the flavor of what is being said.

Mans' Process Of Developing The Answer:

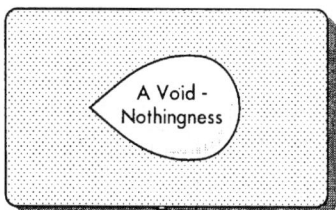

Step #1

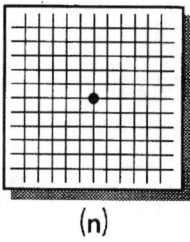

(n)

Philosophers say, "I think, therefore I am." Philosophers attempt to tackle the concept of man the entity; man has value. Mathematicians develop the concept of a point $x = n$, where n represents an infinite number of numbers, an infinite number of locations, points, each infinitely small but each, in turn, infinitely important. Each taken singularly seeming to have little importance, but taken as a whole, having infinite importance. Thus it is with man and thus an infinite number of locations for souls.

Step #2

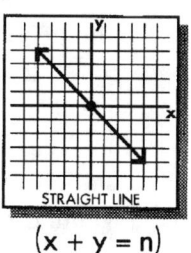

$(x + y = n)$

Philosophers recognize time and ask, "Why?" Astronomers study time to seek out the answer. Mathematicians develop the concept of time with the formula $x + y = n$, what's called a linear formula by mathematicians. Man begins to realize and understand his passage through time. We are mortal. Why do we exist? Religions begin to examine and answer the questions.

Step #3

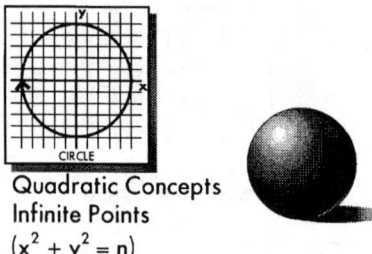

Quadratic Concepts
Infinite Points
$(x^2 + y^2 = n)$

Here is where we begin to lose religion. Here is where religion begins to stagnate. Here is where religion is just now realizing it has stood still for more than a thousand years. Religion orients around one universe. All religions still have not fully accepted the concept of other life forms and have not done so because they do not know how to fuse them into their doctrines. This book is intended to help them with that problem without destroying their very essence and identity.

Man begins to realize he is just one entity of many within a vast sea of entities scattered throughout the heavens, the universe. Mathematicians proceed to describe the concept with the formula $x^2 + y^2 = n$. This is what is known as a simple form of quadratics. It describes a circle, to be filled in by scientists with the concept of matter and energy independent of each other, both swirling around within the circle, our universe.

Step #4

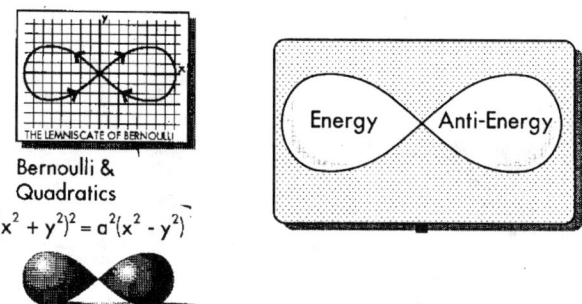

This, then, is followed by the mathematical construction of two independent interiors described by Bernoulli in what is known as "the Lemniscate of Bernoulli". It is described by the formula $(x^2 + y^2)^2 = a^2(x^2 - y^2)$.

Things start to become interesting; complex, yes, but interesting. Sometimes simple things cannot emerge until a lot of pieces of a puzzle are on the table. Once independent portions of the puzzle have been drawn together, one can make sense of what is taking place. Sometimes things have to get complicated before they can become understandable and simple once again.

This concept of Bernoulli's left in a vacuum means little, but once merged with Einstein's concept of the direct relationship of matter and energy, the concept of symmetry by scientists, and the discovery of antimatter by both theoretical mathematicians and physicists, it begins to take on some relevance to man's purpose in the scheme of reality.

Einstein with his concept of $E = mc^2$, begins to fill in the circles with two items, matter and energy. Scientists begin to theorize the filling in of both circles with the unfolding of the concepts of symmetry, energy, matter, and anti-matter, all known today as absolutes in our reality.

Step #5

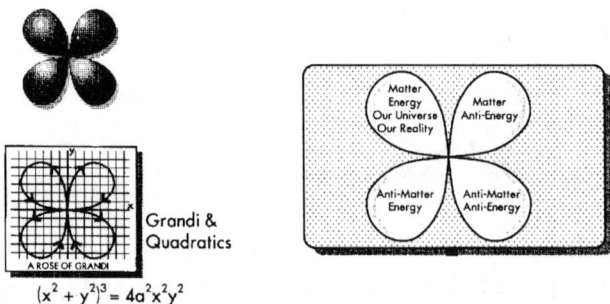

Along comes Grandi, a mathematician with a new twist and the formula $(x^2 + y^2)^3 = 4a^2x^2y^2$. It is called, "a rose of Grandi". How appropriate, for the "rose" is about to be opened by Asimov in his hypothesis of a four leaf clover universe. It is he who hypothesizes the symmetry of anti-energy to complete the disclosure of the configuration of our universe as actually four in one. But the age old question of, "Why" still remains, continuing to haunt man and men.

Step #6

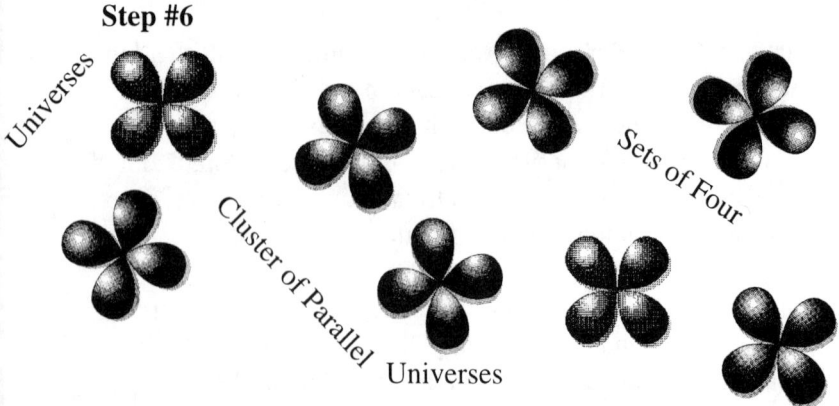

Now with the concept of **sets of four parallel universes** being established as an interesting thought, another concept emerges: why not many sets of parallel universes? But still the haunting question lingers, "Why?"

Religion continues to linger, continues to struggle with the seemingly contradictory discoveries of mathematics/science, mythology, man's deja vu, and new philosophies. What is it going to do to catch up? Fortunately, men are attempting to propel religion into the forefront of leadership once again by modernizing its concepts. Unfortunately for us, for all men, men of religion are attempting to modernize religion through conformity, a process that will, in the end, destroy religion itself and harm man's very purpose, his quest, his journey, through reality. They are burning down the very homes of the souls themselves, but this is dealt with in more detail in the section, **"Christianity/Religions"**.

Yes, cooperation between religions is necessary. Yes, tolerance between religions and men is necessary. Yes, we are all brothers. But this does not mean we all want to live in the same home. It does not mean we all want to look the same way, feel the same emotions, or do the same things. Conformity is not the solution; understanding who we really are and what our purpose in reality is, is the solution.

Is man doing this intentionally? No, rather it is through ignorance. Man has no concept of what his true purpose in life is. Man takes action with no farsighted understanding of who he really is. He sees himself and others as men, not souls, and does not truly conceptualize what the purpose of the soul is.

This is the purpose of this book. Man's purpose in life is what we must formalize, learn, and then accept into our hearts.

It is said that only teenagers seek to be independent and unique through conformity. Well, man is in his teenage years and it is time to wake up and realize this fact. It is time to grow up and realize we have work to do and start getting serious about it.

Now comes the time to develop and expand upon the concepts that will lead us to a more logical understanding of why we should be tolerant, why we must be tolerant, and just where we are going as a species. It is time to stand up once again and ask, "Why?", "Why are we here?", "What is our purpose in this reality?", "What is my purpose in this reality?", "**So, what's the point of it all?**" For now, we have enough information to gain rudimentary insight into the true in-depth answers to these questions.

And with this information we can, with the dual circles of Bernoulli, the concepts of Einstein, the flower of Grandi, and the hypothesizing of Asimov begin to unfold the flower of mankind. We can begin to visualize the beauty of all men. We can begin to answer the age old question of all men and begin for the first time in our history as men to appreciate the logic as well as the full implications in the concept of: "Yes, you really do have a soul", "Yes, you really do have a purpose in life and it is . . .", "Yes, we are all truly brothers", and "Yes, God does exist and WE are HE!"

Now let's begin to take a more detailed look at the concept beginning with Asimov's four sets of parallel universes.

"the philosophy" 51

B.E.G.A. Begins

**Bernoulli, Einstein, Grandi, Asimov
Lead Us Here**

"In Summary"

A Point/The Point

It Took A Lot Of Sweat By Mankind
To Get To B.E.G.A.

The Concept Of The Universe Unfolds

Understanding Of Dual Universes Emerges

Four Sets Of Parallel Universes Unfold
Like A Rose

Wake Up And Smell The Roses

Don't Tear Down My House

Chapter 4: Sets of Four Parallel Universes

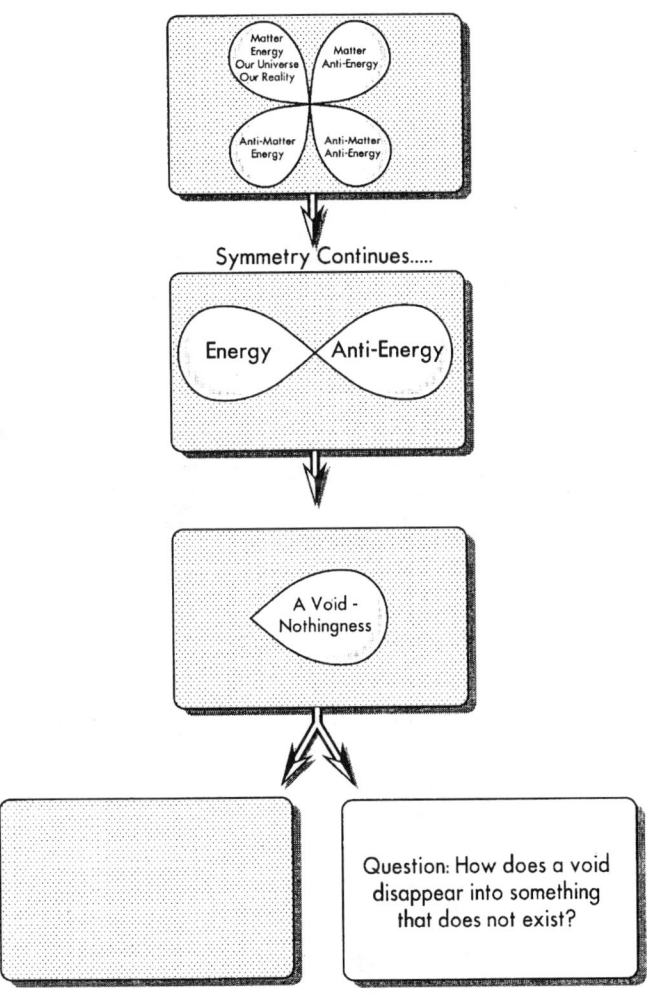

For with God nothing shall be impossible.
Gospel According to Saint Mark

Sets of Four Parallel Universes
♦
From Bernoulli To Grandi With A Twist Of Asimov

Asimov had an interesting theory he set forth in his book *One, Two, Three Infinity*. He said it was possible if the basic principle of physics, symmetry, was correct and is the rule of our universe, then our "universe" is not "the" universe. Rather it is only one of four pieces fit together to form a more probable universe shaped much like a four leaf clover, each leaf being composed by what our present perceptions call a "universe".

Symmetry - The Foundation of Modern Science
Four Parallel Universes

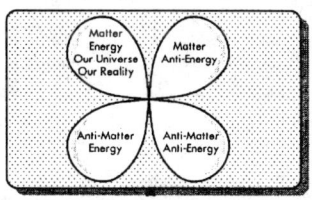

Ours is a universe composed of matter and energy. It makes up one leaf of the clover. A second leaf is composed of anti-matter and energy. We know anti-matter exists. It has already been theorized by mathematicians and scientists. In addition, it has already been found and observed scientifically. According to Asimov, if these two universes got together, they would destroy each other and leave nothing but pure energy – no matter. The matter would have been converted entirely to energy. Now we know that matter, when it comes into contact with anti-matter, does just that. We have observed this reaction in the laboratory. Thus two leaves of this "universe" could annihilate each other to form energy.

What keeps the universes apart? According to Asimov, a barrier similar to the vapor barrier between a drop of water and a hot skillet. A vapor barrier forms between the two and keeps them apart, keeping the drop of water from immediately vaporizing as it dances across the hot skillet.

We have now addressed the principle of symmetry for matter and anti-matter, but it leaves us short regarding energy. Where is the symmetry for energy? Asimov said it would have to lie in a concept we have not found yet – anti-energy.

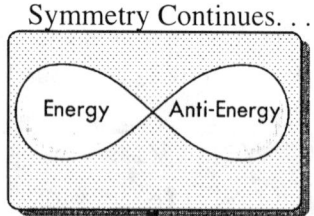

This would require the formation of the other two leaves of the four leaf clover. Of these two leaves, one would be composed of matter and energy and the other of anti-matter and anti-energy. If these two leaves came together, they would entirely annihilate the matter and anti-matter leaving nothing but anti-energy.

This would leave nothing but energy and anti-energy. Asimov then said that the two, if merged, would leave total annihilation. In other words, a void, complete emptiness. A true lack of anything but nothingness.

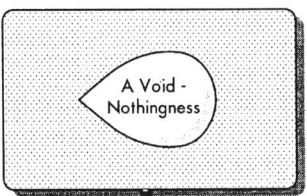

Now this may be interesting, but what could this have to do with philosophy, religion, or God? Everything. For if everything can be transformed into nothingness or a void, then it would seem to follow that everything we know could have been created from nothing or a void. In other words, God as we conceive of Him could have created the Universe.

Why would He do that? What possible purpose could the creation of four universes have to a God – an **omniscient** being?

That is the issue to be delved into in the next topic, "The Universe: One of many Laboratories for Creative Thought".

Sets Of 4 Parallel Universes

From Bernoulli To Grandi With A Twist Of Asimov

"In Summary"

Matter/Energy + Anti-Matter/Energy Equals Pure Energy

Matter/Anti-Energy + Anti-Matter/Anti-Energy Equals Pure Anti-Energy

Energy + Anti-Energy Equals Absolute Nothingness

Absolute Nothingness Is That – Nothingness

Nothingness Is The Lack Of ALL Things Including Emptiness

Thus From Nothingness Comes Something: Us

Four "Universes" Make A Universe

Chapter 5: The Universe

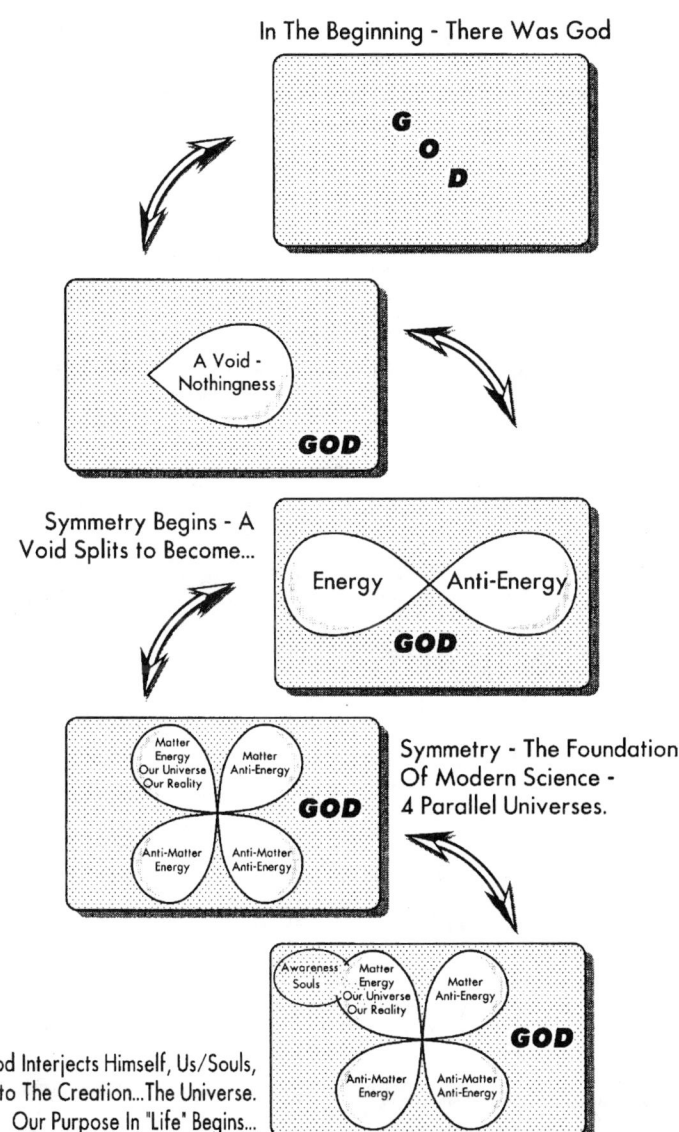

> "What novelty is worth the sweet monotony where everything is known, and loved because it is known?"
>
> George Eliot (1819 – 1880)
> English writer

The Universe
♦
One of Many Laboratories for Creative Thought

If God is omniscience, He would know everything there is to know or could be known at any particular time. This can be true at the same time as being false, thus allowing God the ability of knowing everything while at the same time not knowing much compared to what could be known. This allows the Omniscient the ability of being able to grow in knowledge.

Let me explain. Suppose God exists. Suppose God knows everything there is to know in the universe. He might find existence to be a little uninteresting since He knew everything. Nothing new could come about. He would have no challenges. Not much of an existence. Suppose He wished to be able to add new dimensions to His consciousness. Suppose He wanted to add new knowledge to His omniscience. How could He do this?

In the Beginning - There Was God

How about by creating a void within His **omnipresence**. How does He do this? Simple; He just pries open a place in His consciousness and allows nothing to enter it or in other words, He creates a void. He could thus create as many voids as He wished.

How does this help increase His dimension of consciousness and add new ideas and information to His omniscience? "It" doesn't. What does is what follows. At this point, He could then implement the reverse of what Asimov theorized as the annihilation of four parallel universes and thus create, from nothingness, four parallel universes within each of the innumerable voids.

Symmetry Begins: A Void Splits to Become. . .

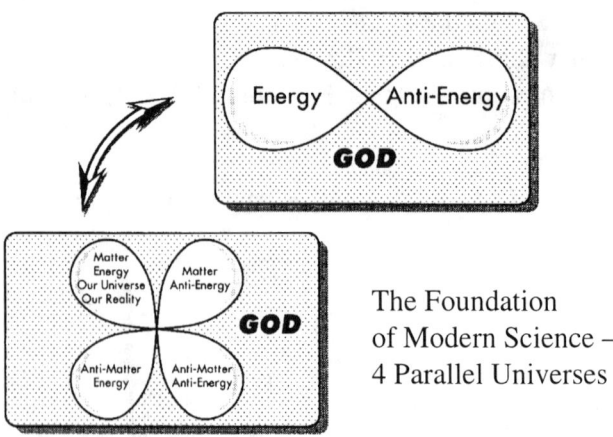

The Foundation
of Modern Science –
4 Parallel Universes

By using an extension of Asimov's Theory of four parallel universes, He would be creating from nothing four universes composed of matter, anti-matter, energy, and anti-energy. Now once these parallel universes were created, He would need to place within them some form of intelligence. To do this He would allow a piece of Himself to transpose itself into the realm of the universe. This would be what we call awareness, the soul. It would take up residence somewhere within the universes and could occupy multiple locations within the universe at one time. He would send each soul with not only a purpose (predestined) but with free-will. In addition, the soul would have to be totally unaware of its origination and its true essence.

God Interjects Himself, Us/Souls, Into the Creation...

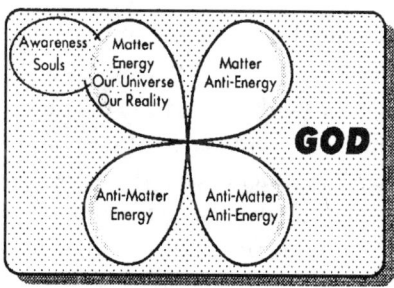

In some cases, **predestination** might or might not exist in the sense of a specific mission to accomplish as we conceive of it today. Most commonly, the soul's predestined purpose would be to learn and experience new things, which it would reveal to God when it fused, after "death", back again into being a part of God.

The free-will would be needed or else the knowledge to be gained or created by the souls sent would have been predetermined, or in other words, already known by the Creator looking for new knowledge and concepts upon which He would like to expand His omniscience. Or to put it another way, not allowing free-will would just defeat the purpose of creation in the first place.

Now comes the difficult part, sending a portion of Himself many times over into universes created in voids within His consciousness. To accomplish His purpose would require the portion of Himself He sent to be both unable to prove its true tie to the Creator or absolutely aware of its true origin. This presents a problem, however, and that is one of deja vu of the soul and God's connection. Thus comes the concept of God, the Creator, the Great Spirit, Allah, etc. since the beginning of Man.

God was just not able to totally isolate Himself from Himself (man and other intelligent beings in the universes) through this process since the soul was in essence a portion of Him or thus Him, was surrounded by Him since the universes were located within His consciousness, and would end up back as Him again, thus the existence of a strong sense of deja vu. The whole concept also allows for other concepts such as **omnipresence** and also Einstein's concept of curved light rays and a bounded universe.

Hold onto your seat for your significance is about to become insignificant but phenomenally grand at the same time. This brings us to the universe itself in the next section, "The Universe: Limitless Limits".

The Universe

One Of Many Laboratories For Creative Thought

"In Summary"

"the universe" Is Not The Universe

Omniscience Is Not Omniscience

Creativity Isn't Confined To Our Universe

Predestination Defeats Its Own Purpose

Our Universe Has An Outside

Even God Needs A Lab

Chapter 6: The Universes

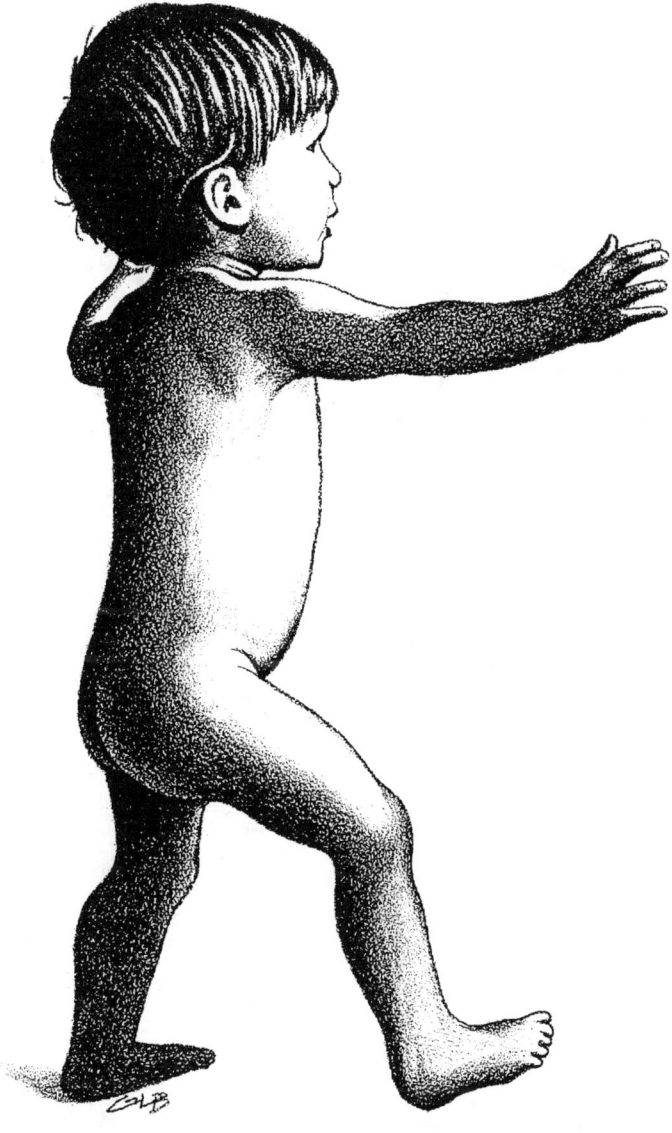

*Heaven is eternal and Earth
everlasting
They can be eternal and everlasting because they
do not exist for themselves,
And for this reason can exist
forever.*

Lao-tzu (c. 604 – 531 B.C.E.)
Chinese philosopher
Founder of Taoism

The Universes
♦
Limitless Limits

Einstein was a firm believer in the concept of our universe having a boundary. This idea, however, was not given serious consideration for a long time and, even today, it is not widely acknowledged as a feasible idea.

The problem is, if the universe has a boundary, then there is a limit, a boundary, to our reality. If Einstein is correct, this tends to corroborate Asimov's concept of "Four Universes in One" making up a complete universe. This in turn would allow for a myriad of universes surrounded and bounded by "something". How frightening for many individuals and how threatening to many of our most economically lucrative and powerful institutions. These two groups have managed to work in conjunction, and each has positioned themselves on opposite flanks of Einstein's idea. They have compressed the idea into a small kernel of creative thought waiting to bloom just as these two groups did to the concept of the Earth orbiting the Sun nearly 400 years ago.

Then there is the dilemma of the boundary itself. A boundary implies a limit and a barrier. This implies something being on the other side. In the past, no one has had any suggestions as to what could possibly be on the other side.

Logic would suggest that if our universe is indeed bounded, and if our universe is basically empty space, then it is a small leap to the concept that we could actually be in a bubble, or basically a void surrounded by an omnipresence, an intelligence, a consciously aware omnipresence. What other logical reason could be given for an "omnipotent omnipresent omniscience" allowing the bubble to survive, other than the fact that the bubble would have a purpose. And what other reason could be more important to an "omnipotent omnipresent omniscience" than the development of new knowledge. Knowledge not just of concrete reality but also of emotional, conceptual, behavioral, artistic realities or fantasy realms.

This would also explain the basic premise of Physics regarding symmetry, which could very well explain the reason for the existence of anti-matter, and the theoretical concept of the unconfirmed anti-energy.

This would allow for the simultaneous four-leafed universe. It would allow for myriad existences of these universes. It would allow for the universal belief in an afterlife, a heaven above and a hell below, eternal suffering for one's sins and eternal reward for one's good deeds.

What, however, does it do for man as a species? Well, for one thing, it definitely should humble us. We are not the only significant life form on earth. For that matter, we would be fairly certain we are not the only significant life forms in the universe. We are not irreplaceable as a species. We need, therefore, to do all we are capable of doing to make sure we maintain our existence as a species and that we ensure our place in eternity as a species by recognizing our purpose and striving to fulfill this purpose.

The significance of this is that in order to accomplish our purpose, we will have to accept the insignificance of ourselves as a species, but at the same time recognize that we can increase our significance as a species if we accept the potential of each and every individual. We must recognize that each of us has the potential to make a contribution to our purpose as a species. We must recognize that as a species we cannot afford to waste the potential of any individuals, for in our case the sum contribution of the whole will truly be greater than the sum of each individual.

We must not passively stand by watching our fellow brothers and sisters suffer, stagnant, vegetate, and fall short of reaching their full potential. We as individuals have a purpose and we as a species have a purpose. We must strive to fulfill our purpose and help others do the same.

Does this mean we have a limit to our universe? Certainly. It does not imply a limit to our existence or number of total Universes, however. Rather it implies a limitlessness for us and other universes. Even more, it means we will once again become absorbed back into God, and once again become God.

Some say we come into this world naked and will leave the world naked. How wrong they are! Although we may come into this world naked and leave this world physically naked, we will not leave this world consciously naked. We will carry with us a conscious awareness not only of our actions, but of the ripple effect these actions had upon all conscious entities. This knowledge will follow us into eternity. We will fully comprehend just how we actually, as individuals, managed to expand upon or stymied the growth of God Himself. The God who in fact is none other than ourselves and our fellow beings who in essence are us.

This leads us to the concept of God Himself having to experience Hell, which then leads us to the next topic, "**The Ripple Effect**" and how it will wash over each and every one of us.

Universes
Limitless Limits

"In Summary"

Man As A Fetus Develops In A Bubble

Our Universe Is A Bubble

Parallel Universes Exist As Bubbles

We Cannot Continue To Exist As An Intelligent Species In A Bubble: We Must Grow Up

Chapter 7: The Ripple Effect

"He who passively accepts evil is as much involved in it as he who helps to perpetuate it. He who accepts evil without protesting against it is really in cooperation with it."

Martin Luther King, Jr. (1929–1968)
American civil rights leader
Stride toward Freedom

The Ripple Effect
♦
Hedonism, Religion, Responsibilities

Understanding the concept of man's purpose in life and living it are two very different things. In order to understand this concept, one must understand that all of one's personal decisions must be predicated upon realizing that the end of life is not the end, rather it is just the return to the beginning. It is the return to true consciousness of a greater reality from whence we came originally. We were injected here with a purpose, and we will return from whence we came for a reason.

In order to live this concept, we have to attempt to be conscious of it at all times. I say "attempt" for we are all "human" and by definition that means we are going to make mistakes. One has to consider "the philosophy" before taking any personal actions, whether it be major personal decisions in life, such as whom one will marry, what medical treatments one will personally accept, what religion one will follow, or whether it be how we interact with our fellow man and our environment. One must realize that all our actions will effect not only ourselves, and those in direct contact with us, but also thousands of others through the ripple effect.

The number of permutations of possible actions by a human life and the resultant interactions of the ripple effect are almost infinite. Therefore, each of us as individuals will have a unique set of experiences, mental pictures, and emotional composites to bring back to the "Omnipotent, Omnipresent Omniscience".

We must, therefore, live our lives realizing that even our smallest actions will have major ramifications upon others. This can lead to a ripple effect sometimes greater than our own major life decisions, without our even knowing it. The simple act of cutting in line or being rude to a customer at work can be "the last straw to break the camel's back" for the person affected by our action. Those actions can then lead someone we affected directly, or more probably through the ripple effect, to commit spousal abuse, child abuse or other negative actions towards others. It may, on the other hand, simply be the beginning of a series of ripple effects that may die off shortly or it may fall into a simultaneous wave reinforcement pattern that could lead to a major worldwide disaster such as in the creation of another Hitler or Stalin.

On the other hand, the reverse can be true. Our smallest actions can lead to a positive ripple effect without our even knowing it. The simple act of saying hello, opening a door with a smile, or offering to help, may be the action that will lead a person to reciprocate in like to others. It may lead to someone responding with a smile to 5 or 6 others, spending more time with their child, or reaching out to their spouse who in turn will reach out to others. It may lead to the beginning of a series of ripple effects that may die off shortly or it may in turn fall into a simultaneous wave reinforcement pattern that could lead to a major worldwide benefit such as in the development of another Lincoln, Ghandi, or Steven Hawking. This concept is too much to bear. It is too much of a burden to shoulder alone. One cannot possibly be worried about how each action we take or do not take will affect all of mankind. We are, after all, only "human". This is a crucial statement. It is realistic. It forces us to accept our limitations while recognizing our significance in the scheme of things. What is one to do then? How can we possibly realize a means of living a life without being so overburdened with responsibility that we literally break?

The answer is not as complex as it would seem to need to be. It has already been established by various philosophers, many of whom seem to be at extreme ends of the spectrum from each other, but when placing the spectrum of behavior in a circle rather than a straight line, are actually very complimentary to each other. The means to finding a way of accepting this philosophy and still maintain peace within oneself is threefold.

1. Hedonism

One needs to accept the fact that one cannot live other people's lives for them. One must live one's own life, seek one's own purpose in life, and one's own source and direction to one's own inner peace. In other words, one must follow one's own path in life, and each of us is capable of sensing only our own direction in life through following our personal inner voice. The voice is loud and clear. It tells us when we are at peace and where peace lies. One need only to train oneself to hear that voice.

We need as individuals to use caution here, however. We must hear the true voice within ourselves and not the voice of convenience and the voice attempting to give us an easy out from our problems.

This then also necessitates the need to recognize and accept the fact that others also must do the same for themselves. This is the hard part, for this leads to the need to let others follow their calling, even if it means they do not attend to our own needs and personal desires. This is easy to say, but difficult to accept and do.

In addition, another difficult action arises for some. This is the realization that we must do what we need to in life for ourselves and not others. Yet we must have the strength to follow our own path and let others do the same without being offended, possessive, remorseful, or hurtful. We must do the same for others, or they will not be able to accomplish their function in life, which will affect us for eternity. On the other hand, we cannot ignore the needs of others, for we will live with that for eternity. This opens the door to the necessity of the concept of self indulgence – hedonism.

Still the burden is too great, since according to the proposed philosophy, our hedonistic actions, and what's worse its ripple effect, will follow us into what is truly eternity. This then leads us to the need for part two.

2. Religion

There are so many actions one can take in life, so many decisions, that a man cannot possibly know which to follow. Which action is selfish and will cause pain, which action will lead to new knowledge and experiences that will create growth of our very souls. We do not know which actions will lead to the creation of a positive ripple effect or which actions will lead to the creation of a negative ripple effect.

Being human, it is too much for us to know. It is too much for us to contemplate regarding each of the millions of actions and reactions we take every day. It is just too overwhelming. Thus enters religion. It is a sanctuary to which we can go to rest our very souls. It is a guide to which we can turn in times of doubt. It is a manual to which we can lead our children whom we ourselves guide, model for, love, empathize with, and through whom we have historically placed our physical mortality.

Religion is a necessity for inner peace. It is necessary for filling the hole of our human lack of knowledge. It is a necessity for accepting our very humanness.

What religion? Does it matter? Definitely. It must be a religion that gives us peace. It must fit our soul. Is this Christianity? Is this Judaism? Islam? No, no, no to all. It is what fits you as a person, as a human being with your own needs and your own particular characteristics. It may be Christianity for you, Judaism for another, Islam for another, etc., etc., etc.

Follow your heart. Follow your needs. Follow the call for inner peace. Too many people today feel their religion is the only way. They are intolerant of the needs of the souls of other people. Because one religion or another tends to dominate geographical regions, people, with differing needs than the religion in dominance, tend to feel lost, as if they are misplaced in life, and indeed they are. Often their misplacement feels geographical.

Their misplacement feels geographical in nature because they don't feel they fit into a region. This in a sense is true, not because of geography – but rather because of society. They are misplaced by other souls attempting to dominate and force what works for them on these vulnerable isolated souls they surround and outnumber. This resistance to submission of the soul is resisted by the very essence of the being involved.

The remedy to the problem is simple but complex. The simple part is to let your soul go and seek out its home. Let your soul find the sanctuary where it feels what's right for it. Let your soul come to roost where it finds peace and then be at peace. The complex part is to get society to become tolerant of others and their ideas and needs. Society must stop ramming its perceptions down the throats of others. Society must stop believing its beliefs, traditions, and morality are the way and the only way.

Does this mean **missionary work** must stop? No, quite the contrary. If people are to find the sanctuary of peace, they must be exposed to as many sanctuaries as possible. I said exposed to, not coerced into accepting the religion that does not fit their soul. Thus missionary work should increase, not decrease. It must not continue to look just away from home but also at home. It must, however, reorient itself from conversion to education.

Hedonism and Religion, two steps to lifting the burden of the ripple effect. Still it is not enough. A third item is missing. A third step is needed to complete the process of making the ripple effect bearable.

3. Accepting Responsibilities

Society today is riveted with crime, lust, hedonistic actions, religious intolerance, racism, pornography, social intolerance, impatience, and despair. What is one to do? It seems an impossible task to resolve these issues.

In a sense, it is an impossible task. But yet it really isn't. To solve a problem, one first needs to find its source. This can often be done by identifying its symptoms. Once the symptoms lead you to the source of the problem, then the source can be dealt with. We are all familiar with the symptoms to some degree or other. Many were listed above. Studying these, we need to find one commonality in them all, if we can. One commonality appears to stick out dramatically above the rest: irresponsibility.

The lack of people taking responsibility for their actions seems to be the main culprit for the illnesses within society. Not taking responsibility for their own learning, behavior towards others, respecting property of others, religious training, their own children, their own physical health, their own state of mind, their own tolerance of others, etc., etc.

Responsibility, responsibility, responsibility!!!

Recognizing the problem leads to a simple solution. People simply need to take responsibility for their responsibilities. Society needs to foster this and not foster submissive dependency and tolerate irresponsibility. Society must stop making excuses for others and stop allowing others to make excuses for themselves. Society must stop accepting excuses about why individuals, groups, and society itself is not responsible for itself.

This sounds like intolerance. How can this fit into a philosophy that calls for the intolerance of intolerance? In a sense it is intolerance but, on the other hand, it is a recognition of the importance of each individual and the soul. It is a recognition of the significance of each life entity, no matter what their economic status, social level, physical appearance, emotional state, or religious belief. Therefore, if one's definition of intolerance is the intolerance of intolerance, then so be it. Many would say, however, it is quite the opposite.

These three items, Hedonism, Religion, Accepting Responsibilities, provide us with the means of finding the frightening concept of an eternal ripple effect to be something we can cope with. This might be a good time to pause and take a small side trip in order to examine a haunting question that may be lingering in the back of your mind. What if the universe implodes or contracts as suggested by scientists? Will it all have any meaning in the end?

The "Ripple Effect"

Hedonism, Religion, Responsibilities

"In Summary"

Our Actions Have A Ripple Effect

Ripples Of Life Will Follow You Into Eternity

Hedonism Does Not Conflict With Religion

Religion Is The Comfort Of The Soul

Responsibility
Responsibility
Responsibility

Chapter 8: The Mechanism

"If I'm ever to reach any understanding of myself and the things around me, I must learn to stand alone. That's why I can't stay here with you any longer."

Henrik Ibsen (1828 – 1906)
A Doll's House, act IX

The Mechanism

What Happens When the Universe Implodes

The creation of a multitude of labs is an interesting concept. But the understanding of the principle of the individual laboratory's stability and what happens to it and the space time continuum it occupies, if it should implode, is an interesting part of this philosophy. The understanding of the true nature of this problem is in its infancy and much speculation can be interjected here and no one would be presumptuous enough to say, "This is how it works." With this established, let's expand and summarize the concept put forth in this book.

There are four sequential steps to be addressed and summarized here:

1. the Creation process

2. the process that stabilizes the present form of our universe

3. the result when the stabilization form collapses

4. the why: what is the purpose of the whole process to begin with.

Let's take a look at each briefly. We'll leave the in-depth examination to others should they determine it merits the effort needed.

1. The Creation Process:

The Universe has been shown by Asimov to be, in theory, able to be destroyed. This implies that it could be created. The mechanism for creating such an immense (in our perspective) body is, at this point, way beyond our comprehension. The reason for its creation is not.

It is not the mechanism of creation itself that is important to man at this point in his development. What is important to man is the reason for the creation. This is what will unite all men and provide the "**missing link**" to mans' understanding of himself as a species and as an individual. Man has a tremendous ability to think, reason, and speculate. He has been doing this, as far as we can determine, since the beginning of His conscious awareness. Putting this accumulated speculation, creative thinking, and reasoning ability together, one can come up with some interesting conclusions.

2. The process that stabilizes the present form of our universe:

The mechanism of the stability of the four parallel universes has been briefly touched upon in the section: **"Sets of four parallel universes"**. The four Universes may be kept apart by a similar process as the means by which a drop of water is kept off a hot griddle. As Asimov suggests, a vapor barrier of sorts may be an insulating and repelling force that keeps the universes apart.

In addition, the universes might act similarly to a balloon. The galaxies, stars, gasses etc., may be acting just as air does in the balloon. The pressure needed to keep the balloon inflated comes from the energy of the molecules of air in the balloon. As the energy of each molecule increases, the molecules increase in motion causing the balloon to expand. As the molecules lose energy, they decrease their motion and the balloon decreases in size.

Expanding or contracting universes, the curvature of light, a curved universe, a bounded universe, a primordial atom, the source of the primordial atom, implosion of the universe, universal noise throughout all of space; all interesting and relatively new concepts in the study of the skies. Perhaps with a more universal picture of man's and mans' purpose in the scheme of things, we can better understand what is truly going on in the heavens above us.

3. The result when the stabilization process collapses:

Matter/energy and anti-matter/energy become energy; matter/anti-energy and anti-matter/anti-energy become anti-energy. Energy and anti-energy become nothing. NOTHING.

Even emptiness is something. We are talking about nothing here. That would call for a total return to the creator.

4. The why: what is the purpose for the whole process to begin with?

The purpose must be significant, otherwise what importance would it have? If the Creating Force were omnipotent, omniscience, and omnipresent with no opportunity to expand its' power, knowledge, or presence, then nothing would have any impact upon the total scheme of existence. But let's say the **Omnipotent, Omniscience, and Omnipresent** were just that but not that. Let's say the Omnipotent, Omniscience, and Omnipresent were able to expand itself, but not through itself directly, since it was omnipotent, omniscient, and omnipresent in the first place. Then to do so would mean it would need a mechanism to do so. That mechanism would be what we recognize as life.

This concept makes no sense if taken in terms of small pieces of mans' up-to-date total individual thoughts. If, on the other hand, we take mans' total up-to-date individualistic thoughts and merge them together and add a few other concepts, we could conceivably come up with the Big Picture. Man's and mans' purpose in life and a crude understanding of the purpose of existence. And nothing, not even annihilation of our physical mechanism can diminish our purpose for existence. Nothing, not even annihilation, can destroy our accomplishments as souls, for they transcend our very physical reality itself.

Just as the universe can destroy itself, so can man. Violence has been an underlying theme in man's history. We have never been able to eliminate it with permanency for any significant lengths of time. Something must be missing. There must be a **"missing link"**.

The Mechanism

What Happens When The Universe Implodes

"In Summary"

- The Creation Process
- The Stabilization Process
- What Happens When The Universe Becomes Unstable
- Why?
- What Possible Reason Could There Be?
- Where Do We Fit In?
- Implosion Will Not Diminish Our Significance

Chapter 9: The Missing Link

> *"What each man does is based not on direct and certain knowledge, but on pictures made by him or given to him... The way in which the world is imagined determines at any particular moment what men will do."*
>
> Walter Lippmann (1889 – 1974)
> *Public Opinion* (1922)

The Missing Link
♦
Evolution Isn't the Only Subject with a Missing Link

We have now reached a point in our understanding of philosophy, science, and religion to be able to recognize that our myths, faiths, deja vus, philosophies, scientific knowledge, and scientific quests of the unknown have a universal intertwining relationship. We are now beginning to appreciate the idea that these areas of study have not only an overlap, but a significant one at that.

We are beginning to recognize this because we have finally come far enough as a species to have developed these concepts to the point where each now has their spheres of knowledge greatly expanded. Expanded enough, in fact, such that their spheres not only touch each other, but in actuality, overlap significantly. This makes the mental passage from one sphere to another not only possible, but easily and frequently done.

We do not want to waste this time in our existence as a species. This is one of the most dangerous times in our existence as a creative intelligent entity. This is a time when the sphere of scientific knowledge has expanded to the point where mankind is capable of destroying itself through biological, nuclear or mind altering processes.

This is a time when the sphere of scientific knowledge has expanded to the point where mankind is capable of destroying itself in the name of righteousness and faith. The kingdoms of faith have always been at odds with each other but the distances between them has been physically large enough to keep them relatively distant. Even so, they have been at each others throats throughout all of mans' history. Look at Ireland with the Catholics and the Protestants, Bosnia with the Muslims and Christians, the Crusades with the Catholics and the Muslims, the inquisition with the church within itself, World War II with the Aryans and the Jews, the settlement of the Americas with the annihilation of the total original civilizations here. These conflicts have not just taken place in the West but have gone on for thousands of years in the East as well.

These conflicts have not taken place between just faiths but between myths, deja vus, and philosophies. It has also taken place not just within each of these realms of mankind individually, but between each of these realms themselves. Major "intra" as compared to "inter" conflicts regarding these realms have been recurrent throughout mans' history. Politics vs. religion – the Communist empire; Christianity vs. scientific knowledge – the inquisition; and philosophy vs. the state – the East/West modern day conflict. These are just a few of the myriad of examples throughout mans' history.

In the past, these conflicts have taken place over a relatively large body of territory and each conflicting party has been slightly insulated from the other. Minor conflicts did occur within the isolated spheres as each concept struggled to maintain its dominance and existence within that territory.

Now, however, through the expansion of scientific knowledge, numerical increase of the human population, and technology, these relatively large territories of insulation are gone and the spheres of conflict are overlapping significantly. This is a dangerous time for mankind. Either we will learn to become tolerant of each other, through tolerance alone, or the historical struggle for dominance will continue. Historically, the creation of an equilibrium of dominance has always been accomplished through violence. The last major episode cost the lives of fifty million lives and was known simply as WWII.

Tolerance for tolerance sake has never in the history of mankind been able to sustain itself. Tolerance has won out for relatively short spans of time – tens, hundreds, even occasionally close to a thousand years, but in the end, tolerance for tolerance sake was not enough, and the close proximity of conflicting thoughts always finally lead to explosive violence and suffering of the individual and man as a whole.

Periods of peace often lead to great explosions of knowledge and culture but often ended up in periods of stagnation of mankind. True, the period of vioience also often lead to great explosions of knowledge and culture, but they too often ended up in periods of stagnation of mankind. These up and down cycles of mankind have to stop. It is too dangerous for mankind as a whole to continue such actions. We have come too far in our knowledge, too numerous in our numbers, and too lucky in our avoidance of large natural calamities to continue these cycles.

How do we manage to break them? Tolerance for tolerance

sake has never managed to accomplish this. Tolerance is necessary, no doubt, but tolerance cannot be the building block to accomplish this feat. The building block that is missing is the step that precedes tolerance in man's and mans' thought process, reasoning process, and understanding process. This step is a universal understanding of man and mankind's purpose in the scheme of the universe. It is this step that will lead us to understand all the mysteries of our faiths, myths, deja vus, and deep seated desire to expand our scientific knowledge. It is this step that will act as the cementing compound which will bind man to man, mankind, and other intelligent life forms that we will surely find as a species as we begin to explore the universe beyond our solar system.

Pity mankind and extraterrestrial life forms if we are unable to find this universal binding agent for our species. If we fail to find this universal binding agent, one of two things will surely happen: one, we may self destruct our present level of development through our historical pattern of violence. This level of violence has been increasing geometrically in intensity as we have increased our knowledge base. This self destruct process will not be pleasant or insignificant. Or two, heaven help us, we will make it into the stars and continue our conflict there as we did in the Americas and other places in and on this good earth.

I believe we have enough creativity as a species to develop this step, this universal understanding of man and mankind's purpose in the scheme of the universe. Steven Hawking gave us some possible direction to look when searching for this "universal philosophy" when he said, "If we do discover a complete (unified) theory (of the universe), it should in time be understandable in broad principle by everyone, not just a few scientists. Then we shall all, philosophers, scientists, and just ordinary people, be able to take part in the discussion of the question of why it is that we and the universe exist. If we find the answer to that, it would be the ultimate triumph of human reason – for then we should know the mind of God."

Perhaps it is time we begin this quest. This book is an attempt to do just that. "The philosophy" has been outlined and established. Now comes the test Steven Hawkings indicates a universal philosophy needs to pass: an ability of all men to comprehend it.

In addition, a universal philosophy should be able to resolve problems of man the individual and mankind as a social species in terms of the past, present, and future. In other words, a universal philosophy needs to be put to the test and that is just what section II, "The Impact" attempts to do. But before we move into this realm, let us show a little more patience and examine the concept of God, the creator, having limits to Himself, in a little more depth. This will be done in the next section: "Omnipotent/Omnipresent/Omniscience", Man Playing God.

The Missing Link

Evolution Isn't The Only Subject With A Missing Link

"In Summary"

Mans' Spheres Of Ideas Now Overlap

Man At The Point Of Self Destruction

Mankind Has Always Ended Up Solving Major Conflicts With Violence

Past Historical Cycles Of Violence Must Stop

Tolerance Is Not Enough

Man Must Find A Way To Bond To Man

Something Is Missing

Let's Find It

Chapter 10: Omnipotent/ Omnipresent/ Omniscience

Flower in the crannied wall,
I pluck you out of the crannies,
I hold you here, root and all, in my hand,
Little flower – but if I could understand
What you are, root and all, and all in all,
I should know what God and man is.

Alfred Lord Tennyson (1809 – 1892)
Flower in the Crannnied Wall (1869)

Omnipotent/Omnipresent/Omniscience
♦
Man Playing God

What true monotony it must be to be all-powerful, be everywhere at the same time, and know everything there is to know or ever will be known.

The three ultimate paradoxes of all paradoxes:

1. knowing everything there is to know, will ever be known, or could be known; being everywhere within all time frames; and being all powerful but not being able to change a thing

2. being all powerful; knowing everything there is to know, will ever be known, or could be known; and being everywhere within all time dimensions but being held a prisoner within your own time frames

3. being everywhere within all time frames; being all powerful; and knowing everything there is to know, will ever be known, or could be known, but not knowing you do not know

everything.

Ah man, what an egotistical creature we are!

We create paradoxes of life ourselves, give them a life of their own, and then perpetuate their irrationality into absolutism. What a piece of irony we are. Truly we must be made in the image of God. For what other creature would attempt to make its own universal truths; raise them to a level of the laws of nature itself; and then through the power of one word, "faith", would cut short its own natural drive to seek the truths concerning the ultimate of ultimates, its own origin, its purpose in the scheme of things, and its destiny as a creative, curious, thinking species.

Maybe we need to expand our thoughts and start tearing down the many paradoxes we have created and begin replacing them with the realization we do not know everything, including morality. Maybe we need to stop playing God, and begin accepting the fact that we need to start showing more tolerance to others. Maybe we need to provide total support to the individual, respect their decisions, relate to the idea we all face our own dilemmas and therefore need each other to lean on. Maybe we need to stop expending so much personal energy taking responsibility for other people's lives and decisions regarding how to live and start taking care of our own souls.

We have an obligation to reach out to each other and we must protect each other's right to influence our own individual souls. At the same time, however, we must stop interfering with each individual's quest in life to fulfill their own destiny.

In order to do this with any permanency, we must reevaluate the very foundations we have created, the three ultimate paradoxes of paradoxes; omnipotence, omnipresence, and omniscience. We must begin to realize that these concepts were useful at one point in mans' development, but in fact are no longer relevant. We must begin to open our minds, observe our place in history, and recognize that our travel as a species through time has now lead us to a point where we must take a leap beyond the point our leg irons of confinement to this earth will reach.

We cannot do this, however, if we continue to be limited by the concepts of omnipotence, omnipresence, and omniscience. These three words continue to keep us chained to intolerance, attempting to fanatically indoctrinate others into our own personal beliefs; and confined to believing through "faith" alone and rejecting the place of reason in our quest to find the purpose of our own existence and that of all men.

Faith cannot be thrown out the window, nor can morality, spirituality, love, kindness, etc. We cannot throw out what has taken us thousands of years to develop. Our past traditions have a purpose and need to be protected jealously. What generations have nurtured over the millennia cannot in all good conscience be thrown away by one or two generations. This would be the greatest of all insults we could possibly confer upon our fathers before us. Our past beliefs, traditions, faiths, and hopes give us comfort, guidance, and roots. There is nothing that can replace them.

Eliminating the paradox of omnipotence, omnipresence, and omniscience does not alter or call for the elimination of the rich history of traditions or beliefs. It just expands our view of our place in the universe, our purpose in the scheme of things. It allows us to see why we must reach for the stars. It forces us to stop visualizing one man's role in society as more important than another.

Elimination of our present concept of omnipotence, omnipresence, and omniscience does not bring down the foundations of our society. Rather it provides a foundation to our foundation so that we may continue to develop as a species and add to what we already know and to where we have already traveled. Our present foundation is beginning to crack from the weight of the persistent geometrically increasing knowledge we are acquiring and building upon.

Omnipotence, omnipresence, and omniscience paradoxes? Only because we have made them so and continue to perpetuate these concepts.

Why is it that we feel the need to believe that our creator is omnipotence, omnipresence, and omniscience? Could it be just another example of mans' need to be at the center of things? We fought this war before with the pugnacious attempt to let go of the concept that our earth was the center of the universe. Perhaps that was not a war at all; perhaps it was just one more battle in the total war of man's quest for the stars, mans' quest to fulfill his purpose both as an individual and as a species.

Rationalizing a means by which our concept of a creator is able to expand to allow for growth of the creator Himself by no means belittles the power, presence, or knowledge of that creator. Quite the contrary. It actually expands upon the magnitude of that very force and produces an omnipotence, omnipresence, and omniscience that continues to become even more omnipotence, omnipresence, and omniscience all the time while at the same time providing us with a significant role to play in that very development.

How exciting, how marvelous, how awe-inspiring a concept it is that we may actually be an important aspect in the development of an increasingly more omnipotence, omnipresence, and omniscience force. The concept of our playing an important role in this development of this thriving, growing intelligence can do nothing but cause each of us to pause and reflect upon the significance of not just ourselves but of those around us. It would force us each to look in awe upon every man, woman, and child. It would force us to see the sacredness of each and every individual. It would humble each of us in our insignificance, delight each of us in our importance, frighten each of us in our responsibilities, and look upon our fellow men as brothers in life.

In other words, it would force us into a mode of tolerance to each other.

Omnipotence/Omnipresence/Omniscience

Man Playing God

"In Summary"

Three Ultimate Paradoxes Of All Paradoxes

Man Is A Piece Of Irony Himself

Faith And Rationality Go Hand In Hand

Leave Others Alone

You Are Your Brother's Keeper

Man Creates Paradoxes, Not God

One Small Change Can Lead To Unshackling The Chains

Tolerance And Brotherhood, One In Each Hand

Chapter 11: In Summary

All your strength is in your union.
All your danger is in discord;
Therefore be at peace henceforward,
And as brothers live together.

Henry Wadsworth Longfellow
(1807 – 1882)
The Song of Hiawatha (1855)

In Summary

Simply Put

"The philosophy" cannot be understood in total until it is put to the test, which is the purpose of the next section. Man is a paradox, and what may seem to be a worthless life to one person may in fact be of immense value in the scheme of things. Having put forward the general concept of "the philosophy" in sections 1 through 10, this section will attempt to summarize the overall picture first by chapter and then by impact.

"The philosophy":

1. God "is" and we, man and other intelligent life forms, are He.

2. Linear thought has limited us to an incomplete understanding of our purpose and our place in the blueprint of reality.

3. Man thinks and grows.

4. Using symmetry, God can and did create our universe.

5. Being omniscient, God cannot create original concepts so He created isolated labs to do so.

6. God may have a limitless number of limited labs contained within His omnipresence.

7. Every individual has an infinite amount of effect upon the future and his eternity will be partially devoted to fully understanding and living with "his" true impact.

That's it. Seven of the ten chapters says it all. Chapters 8 through 10 attempt to clarify:

8. Reiteration of 1 – 7 from a slightly different perspective.

9. Beginning an explanation of the impact of "the philosophy".

10. Three paradoxes that keep man shackled.

The impact:

"The philosophy" is rather simple, the impact is profound. The impact is too influential in all areas of man's life to explain in Book I outlining "the philosophy". Therefore in order to do it justice, "the impact" itself will be given a significant section in order to attempt to begin to express its overall influence upon man, religion, society, the future of man, and mans' next step in his development – mans' leap into the heavens.

"The philosophy" and its impact are an attempt to develop a simplistic universal philosophy, an understanding of the age-old haunting question – "Why, what's the purpose?", with an impact that would be profound. All this had to be based upon scientific evidence, religious beliefs and mans' past knowledge. In addition, one other element was essential. It all had to be based upon the ancient Greek premise that the most beautiful, the most logical, and the most probable concepts in our reality are the simplest.

"The philosophy" has just seven basic concepts, all listed above. It does nothing, once truly examined in depth, to destroy. It just builds. It just reinforces . It just answers the universal question of "Why, what's the purpose?" Once having answered this question, it opens a new door to mans' and man's quest to find evidence to prove he was not wrong in his struggle over the millennia to follow a particular way of life; to follow philosophies that required self discipline; to follow blindly, leaders he somehow knew were touched by God; to follow his soul when he was never sure his soul even truly existed. All this he did through blind faith. So resolved was he, that he not only managed to do so himself over the countless millennia, but he lead his children in blind faith over the millennia to do likewise. To have done so over such a long period of time had to take much faith, trust, and love. Truly man is a great entity. Surely man must be more than just man.

We are not finished, however. Quite the contrary. We have just begun. Finally we have come to the point in our development where we no longer need to follow faith blindly. We have now come to the point in our development where we can follow our faiths truly knowing they are there to give us guidance. They are there to give us comfort. They are there to give us peace.

Finally, we no longer need to follow our faiths through faith in their correctness, trust in their prophets and leaders, and soul-wrenching attempts to overcome our personal doubts of our undaunting beliefs. We can now see the truths they professed to be are true. We can now make our step into the stars, touch other intelligent life forms while understanding their place in the scheme of reality, seek the wonders of creation while we fulfill our purpose in reality of developing new and exciting concepts ourselves. We are now ready to use this good earth as a base from which we may explore the stars. We may now begin to work as a total unit: blacks, whites, yellows, browns; men, women, children; males, females; big people, little people; intellectuals, mentally deprived; commoners, aristocrats; rich, poor; weak, strong; aggressive, submissive; outgoing, withdrawn; social lights, wall flowers; physically fit, couch potatoes; gifted, plain old Joes; visibly handicapped, and the rest of us who are carrying unobservable handicaps, the **silent crosses**. We are now ready to recognize that all men must participate in life, and all of us must find a means of allowing this to happen in a respectable manner for all men, for all men are truly equal.

We are at the threshold, as a species, of jumping beyond self destruction, realizing our commonality, and becoming brothers in life to work as a team in our next venture. We are at the threshold as intelligent life forms, as literally portions of God Himself, of jumping into the exciting, beckoning, beautiful heavens themselves. The Laboratories of God. Our laboratories. We are so close. We just have that one missing link that is necessary to cement the realization that all men are truly equal into place in order to complete our universal picture of mankind. Perhaps now it does not have to be a missing link any longer.

The second part of this book is intended to put "the philosophy" to work. It is intended to do so through short stand-alone items that when read reinforce the concepts of "the philosophy". They cannot be fully understood without reading "the philosophy" of course, but they can stand on their own for the most part.

The second part of this book is intended to draw people to a portion of the book that may help them come to terms with problems with which they are struggling and find possible comfort with their decisions by giving them an understanding of their purpose in the scheme of reality. Should they have religious leanings, "the philosophy" is intended to reinforce those personal religious convictions they may have should they be of the universal nature man has always sensed existed.

Due to the fact that Part II of this book is intended to be written as stand-alone items giving insight to many conflicts of man as a whole and man as an individual, there will be a certain amount of repetition. To best express the impact of "the philosophy", the second part of this book will be divided into three main concepts:

1. Man: the individual/the species

2. Man's society/the present

3. Man: historical reflections and the future

"The philosophy" will never again allow us to look into another man's eyes or through a mirror into our very own eyes, in the same way. Now whenever we look into another man's eyes, we will realize we are looking into his soul and realize he is truly our equal. We will see the importance of his soul regarding our eternity and the eternity of all men.

We will have a broader insight into our purpose in life and realize, no one, not even ourselves, has the right to interfere with the mission of the soul of another man. Knowing this we will jealously and fanatically work to protect our right AND the right of all souls to seek out the fulfillment of their missions in life. For not to do so will follow us into eternity. God help us all!

"In Summary"

Paradoxes

"the philosophy's" 7 points

The Impact

True Brotherhood

Man Never Again Will Be The Same

"Philosophies, to be useful and not just idle babble, need to be functional. Do not misunderstand, idle babble lead to this concept, therefore idle babble is not of itself useless for it may be idle babble initially, but once unified with other idle babble, it may prove to have much use.

"This paradox is the crux of man's life. Man is a paradox and what may seem to be a worthless life to one person may in fact be of immense value in the scheme of things."

Daniel J. Shepard

Book II:

♦

The Impact Of

"the philosophy"

♦

Putting "the philosophy" To The Test

Part A.

Man

The

Individual

Let's Talk Details

BOOK II: The Impact
A. MAN
The Individual/The Species..........128

Introduction
Man A Machine?..........131

12. **Man's Inhumanity to Man**
    Does no one Rememer? Will Someone
    Please Make it Stop?..........139
13. **Man's Good Side**
    We are our Brother's Keeper..........147
14. **Is it Worth it in the End?**
    Is there Really a Heaven and a Hell?.....161
15. **Is There Hope for You as an Individual?**
    Hope is all we Have..........169
16. **Is There Hope for Mankind?**
    Swirling Waters of the Lack of Conviction
    Continue Eroding Away the Pillars........179
17. **Religion**
    Is it Really Significant /Necessary?.......189

18. **In Summary**
    The Soul..........199

"The soul after death goes nowhere where it has not been from the very beginning, nor does it become other than that which it has always been, the one eternal omnipresent."

Yajnavalkya (4th c. B.C.E.)
Indian philosopher

Introduction
♦
Man a Machine?

Machines are devices created by man to do work for him. They are, granted, simplistic at their present level of development. They are, nonetheless, serving their function and becoming more sophisticated as time goes on. Case in point; look at the development of machines since the beginning of the industrial revolution to the present, and the development of the initial phases of the silicon chip computers leading us into the computer age.

All machines must meet a well thought-out, all-encompassing list of guidelines starting from the point of creative inception to the final phase itself in which the machine has actually fulfilled its purpose and or just worn out.

The very start to finish of well-planned machines follows a specific pattern:

1. a clear conceptualization of the purpose for which the machine must be built

2. a blueprint for the most efficient machine to fulfill that purpose

3. a total plan from beginning to end regarding construction, placement, and functioning of the very machine itself

4. a planned integration of the machine into the total picture of reality.

If we jump into the analogy of comparing ourselves to a form of machine, the process would go somewhat like the following:

Reality before our reality (**God**).

An omniscience, omnipotent, omnipresent force could do anything but it would have to do so within its knowledge, within its means, and within itself. The construction of the environment in which the machine, man, was to function, was completed (**Sets of Four Parallel Universes**). Not only was it completed within the framework specified, it was constructed using knowledge of how to create something from nothing. In addition, it was created through a powerful need and by actually creating voids within itself, since nothing could be created outside an all present being.

Man was created for a purpose (The Universe: **One of Many Laboratories for Creative Thoughts**).

Man is not alone (**The Universe: Limitless Limits**).

And man the machine will not live forever, but the soul will, both as an individual entity and as a part of a whole (**The**

Ripple Effect).

This leads us into the machine and how "a total philosophy" can guide people regarding its use through an insight into the purpose of the entity that is occupying it; your very soul.

This leads us into the impact of "a total philosophy" itself. An impact so profound, no intelligent man would dare ignore it. An impact so clear, no rational thinking being would be able to counter its logic.

Man is a machine. Man is predestined. Man has a soul. The soul is predestined. The soul is not a machine but rather exists within the machine. Neither man nor the soul is predestined in terms of specifics, just in terms of broad generalities regarding the final manner in which the results of the souls' travels within this reality will be used. Man is in a specific reality; the universe.

Man is a machine. Man has free will. Man has a soul. The soul has free will. The soul can never be destroyed. The soul will carry with it the results of its decisions for eternity. The soul has many lives; reincarnation exists. Who knows for sure in what specific manner, but it does exist. Be careful with yourself for you are your soul itself. Be careful with others for they are souls themselves. You are your brother's keeper, for your brother is in essence a soul and was extracted from God Himself and therefore is, in essence, God, just as you are, in essence, a soul and were extracted from God Himself and therefore you also are, in essence, God. You will both return to God again and become as one once again. You both will live with each other and with the effects you had on each other into eternity.

You, as all souls, will become fully aware, in every sense, of your actions within this reality. You will live with these results throughout eternity. This will occur through the ripple effect process and will end up being your very own heaven as well as your very own hell. You will have no one to thank and no one to blame but yourself.

Love? Yes, love. It is the core of all religions. The reason was not previously fully understood, it was just sensed to be. It was followed, not through rational thought but through blind trust in man's intuitive insights, for generation after generation. It was followed as "the" way to conduct one's life. It was accepted through faith, lived through faith, and passed on through faith by man throughout history. Now it is time to move on and add to our present historical and basic intuitive foundation, another foundation.

It is time to add to our present foundation, a foundation that will lead to the acceptance of the tolerance of one's fellow man as a universal principle by which man will live. A principle which religion, science, and mans' past intuition has expressed as valid but which man has been unable to consistently implement.

Man is on the edge of a new millennia and of taking a quantum leap into the stars. We will need a stronger foundation than faith if we are to be freed of our past historical trends as a species. We will need a foundation to support our present foundation if we are to accomplish our purpose as a species as we enter the next age of man. It is time to add a rational understanding of man's and mans' purpose and how it will be accomplished.

It is time to add a foundation, a true understanding, of the concept of the brotherhood of men to men if we are to begin to extend our influence as a relatively intelligent species from this small planet into the immensity of the heavens themselves. By adding bits and pieces of religion, science, and mans' universal intuition, we can form a foundation that not only rationalizes religion, science, and mans' universal intuitions, but makes all men aware of the consequences of their actions and of their actual purpose in life.

This, in turn, will make men not only aware of why they must pursue their own personal fulfillment in life, but why they must also act cohesively as a total unit of men to advance the purpose of man himself. Man must accept the uniqueness of each machine. Man must utilize the special talents, abilities, and contributions of each individual, race, and gender. But this is the recognition of the machine, at the same time man must see the soul within. Man must accept the concept that the machine is not the man, that man is, in actuality, the soul. With this comes the ability to accept each soul as a brother, each soul as truly a part of oneself. Once man accepts all souls as a part of himself, how can man ever again reject another?

"The impact" will explain what, how, and why a specific process, using the concept of the brotherhood of all men as the main guiding light, must be followed by each and all men in regards to their actions towards one another.

"In Summary"

All Machines Evolve To Higher Levels

You Are Not Man

Man Is A Machine

You Are The Soul Within The Machine Of Man

You Have Free Will

YOU Are Responsible For ALL Your Actions

You Will Face Your Own Ripple Effect With No Excuses Allowed

Our Present Foundation Needs A Foundation

An Entity Is Only As Good As Its Foundation

A Few Words Are Worth A Thousand Pictures

Mans' Inhumanity To Man
Does No One Remember?
Will Someone Please Make It Stop?

"A Tear For Man"

*Just a spot on the earth, a mere 40 acres,
in four years, here, at the hand of man;
2,500,000 people are executed;
500,000 starve to death;
100,000's more die in transit to
their crime, being men;
the religious
the religious leaders
the handicapped
the mentally unique
the politically incorrect
and in a set of 27 volumes and 25,000,000 words describing the
world of man and men,
all we have to say is:*

"Auschwitz, OWSH vihts, was one of the most infamous Nazi concentration camps during World War II. It was opened in June, 1940, in Auschwitz (now Oswiecim) in Poland, about 30 miles 49 kilometers from Krakow. In June, 1941, it became an extermination center when four huge gas chambers were installed. Rudolf Hess, who directed the camp for more than three years, testified at the Nuremberg trials that over 2 1/2 million persons were executed at Auschwitz and 500,000 more starved to death. Most of the people who died at Auschwitz were Jews from German-controlled countries."

World Book 1984 Volume I

100 words - no tears

Need anymore be said about mans' inhumanity to man ?

Daniel J. Shepard

"Man's inhumanity to man, Makes countless thousands mourn!"

>Robert Burns (1759 – 1796)
>*Man Was Made To Mourn* (1786)

Chapter 12:
Mans' Inhumanity To Man
♦

Does No One Remember?
Will Someone Please Make It Stop?

The early nineteen hundreds, one and a half million Armenians die because they are what they are: Armenians.

Middle nineteen hundreds, fifty million people die in W.W.II because, as Hitler said to his generals before implementing his plans to annihilate the Jews, "Who, after all, speaks today of the annihilation of the Armenians?" Tens of millions of people die deliberately and directly through the order of their own leaders: Hitler and Stalin.

Late nineteen hundreds, billions of people are held hostage as the ironic twist of using the threat of their annihilation is vocalized as the humanitarian action of the century, the action that will keep the world in peace through the mortification of mankind.

The acceleration from the beginning of the century to the end of the century is not a linear progression, but a geometric one. Where will it go from here if we, as a race, if we as a species, if we as individual men, do not intercede?

Hanging within the periphery of these events and interspersed throughout the century run minor incidences by comparison, such as: gas warfare in World War I; 500,000 Rwandans killed at the hands of their brothers; ethnic cleansing in Yugoslavia; gassing of Kurds in Iraq; China's cultural revolution; 100,000 Hereros in Namibia slaughtered by Germans in the 4 years of 1904–1907. Is this all? By no means, for technology has progressed much further than just being able to accommodate these few incidences.

From the beginning of this century to the end, the blood flows as rivers through the pages of our history. We've become so good at killing others that new techniques of killing become the novelties of our age. Gas chambers, machine gun massacres, poison gas, and biological warfare replace the bow and arrow.

Man has not forgotten, however, his old standbys of torture: man-made famine, mass drowning, death marches, visits in the night, etc., etc., etc. We become so good at what we do, a new term, "genocide", is introduced in a book written by Raphail Lemkin, a Polish born law professor and a Jew who lost family members in the Holocaust. Sadly, the term is not only introduced but absorbed without fanfare into the vocabularies of the world. The world embraces the word not with shock but with quiet acceptance and resignation.

The total estimation of the number of lives snuffed out in the most advanced century of mankind runs into the hundreds of millions. Oh, if only this were the extent of it. But the list moves from mass killings of the masses by the masses to individual killings of individuals by individuals.

Necklacing, the process of soaking a tire in gasoline, placing

The Impact 141

it around a person's neck, and then setting it afire, can now be added to shooting, stabbing, rape, incest, hit men, serial killing. The list, will it ever stop?

Mothers kill their own children; children kill their own parents; husbands kill their wives; wives kill their husbands; neighbor kills neighbor; employee kills boss; customer kills clerk; stranger kills stranger; and on it goes. Will it never end?

Then comes the violence of intimidation intended to strike fear into the hearts of the victim through: stalking, obscene phone calls, law suits, car jackings, breaking and entering, robbery, child abuse, spousal abuse, parent abuse, community ostracism, sexual harassment, ad infinitum. Does it finally stop here? Sadly no, for mans' inhumanity to man then moves into man's inhumanity to himself.

This emerges as drug abuse, alcoholism, self-deprivation, suicide, coccooning, anorexia, smoking, TV addiction, self imposed guilt, gambling addictions, etc., etc. Then to be even more efficient, the ideas and suggestions for: types, techniques, creativity, implementation, detection avoidance, and glorification of violence and the threat of violence has improved. No longer do the methods surrounding violence have to be spread through word of mouth. No longer does the violent act stay localized. With the advent of the mass media: radio, TV, movies, newspapers, magazines, video tapes, and the internet, the capabilities to spread all types of violence has become not only extremely efficient but actually competitive between the media. Competition to be the first and best in their reporting, dramatizing, and selling the product of violence and intimidation sweeps the media like a highly contagious disease.

The past brings us the hundred years wars, Mongol invasions, crusades, inquisitions, child work factories, torture, forced confessions, iron maiden, guillotine, stoning, branding, burning at the stake, ad nausea.

The present brings us necklacing, biological warfare, chemical warfare, internet intimidation, racing, nuclear warfare, 15 minute notification of imminent destruction of millions, incarcinogens, radioactive contamination, ozone depletion, global warming, letter bombings, to mention just a few.

Is it any wonder that so many people are depressed today? Is it any wonder so many people suffer from anxiety attacks? Is it any wonder that people are starting to isolate themselves within the confines of their own homes?

Is it all doom and gloom? Is it all hopeless? Why is the negative accelerating? Is there any hope at all? Something must change, but what?

The past has not shown us the way to reduce this trend of violence and inhumanity of man to man. This problem has increased geometrically throughout time. The medias' drive to be the first with the best and most has lead to the fierce competition to glorify, glamorize, and rationalize the violence and inhumanity. This has lead to an explosion of exposure to the elderly, middle age, and what is truly sad: the teens and children of our society. The impressionable are being indoctrinated to the very behavior that we as a society abhor.

One must wonder – if those producing these media exposures are aware of the fact that they will live the results of their labors for eternity, through the Ripple Effect. No amount of rationalizing or logic will prevent their living through the fruits of their labors. The effects the violence generated by their work will lay as surely on their shoulders as those that committed the acts influenced by the producers of the mass media articles and programs.

We have come to the point where we must finally answer our age old questions: "Who am I?" and "What is my purpose in life?" It is the answers to these two questions that seems to be holding man and mankind up in its quest for true peace: peace of the heart, peace of the soul, peace of man towards man, peace of man to mankind.

With the answers to these two questions, we can finally come to terms with ourselves, come to terms with our very souls, our essence, and accept ourselves and all others as equally important entities in the confines of reality.

Perhaps "the philosophy" will act as a first step to the realization of just who we really are and just what our purpose in life really is. Perhaps a universal philosophy will show man the follies of his ways. Perhaps a universal philosophy will assist him in changing the direction of the speeding locomotive of historical trends away from the continuation of man's inhumanity to man.

Does no one remember? Yes, we do. People just don't understand how to change it. Will someone please make it stop? No, they won't. We must do it ourselves. We must do it ourself. We cannot rely on someone else to do it. Tolerance of all men, acceptance of all men as true equals, understanding of the fact that all men are truly brothers through the soul, through a common purpose in reality, is what will finally unite all men. The realization that we will literally live the effects of our actions during this reality is the only thing that will cause men to pause, reflect, and weigh the results of their actions before taking the actual action.

Answering the questions, "Who am I?" and "What is my purpose in life?" could well lead us to a resolution to the troubled soul. A resolution to the violence. A resolution to man and mankind's uncertainty of his significance in reality. A resolution of man's and mankinds' intolerance of other men, their very brothers in the afterlife.

Men must begin to accept the reality that the actions they take today become their very own living hell tomorrow. Men must begin to accept the fact that they are responsible for their own actions and there will be no one else to shift the responsibilities to and no excuses will remove the results from their own eternity.

Is there hope?

Yes, we can always hope.

Mans' Inhumanity To Man

Does No One Remember?

"In Summary"

Man Is Inhumane To Mankind

Man Is Inhumane To Man

Man Is Inhumane To Himself

We Need To Understand Our Purpose

Understanding Will Lead To True Acceptance Of All Men

Understanding Will Lead To True Acceptance Of Ourselves By Ourselves

No One Can Stop It But You

*"Through many dark hour,
I've been thinking about this,
That Jesus Christ was betrayed by a kiss,
But I can't think for ya,
You'll have to decide,
Whether Judas Escariet had God on his side."*

Bob Dylan
With God On Our Side

Chapter 13:
Man's Good Side

♦

*The Irony Is – Judas Was A Good Man
Take Heart: If Judas Was A Good Man,
There Is Hope For You*

There are many "good" men in this world and many more that are good a lot of the time and even more that are good some of the time.

Good men sometimes are not recognized as such because their actions are not highly visible, or are judged by themselves and others to be ordinary, or are used by other men selfishly to advance their own personal agenda. Unfortunately, these personal agendas are often preconceived within the notion of what's good for man but what proves to be contrary since it is developed within a vacuum, an absence of a total, comprehensive picture of mans' true purpose in this reality.

Men do not understand their true function in life. They have no grasp of what it is they are supposed to be accomplishing in life so they set up their own goals. Most of the time, these goals are short-sighted in light of the vastness of the universe and what exists beyond the universe itself. Many of these short-sighted goals have completely missed "the point of it all" and thus men set the course of their life's actions upon totally erroneous assumptions that they set up for themselves.

This frequently leads to totally erroneous actions. These actions can lead to a spiraling set of negative repercussions coursing throughout the framework of mans' history, the existence of mans' reality itself. These actions can be so broad and extensive in scope that other men are hard pressed to counteract their negative effect.

Let's take a look at a prime example, a look at a good man, a man no worse than you or I. A man that has been so misrepresented that he has been portrayed as one of the most despised, vilified men of the modern history of western culture. Let's look at this man through the eyes of the most powerful moral, cultural, and political institutional organizations established within the last two thousand years: Christian religious institutions. After examining this man through the eyes of the past, let's add a foundation to the religious organizations that they do not presently know exists, "the philosophy", and then re-examine this man again through the eyes of the church sitting upon a new foundation, "the philosophy". Then using the simple concepts of "the philosophy", that man is God, and man has a purpose, let's see how things would change.

Let's do this to see if some "bad" men may be "good", not because they are any different, but because their purpose in life, their identification with other men, has been misconstrued. If this can be done, it will help us come a long way toward looking at our fellow man in a different context. It will help us see more good in the world and realize that there is more to the good side of man than we realize.

Keep in mind that religious organizations were and are made up of men, souls all, and just as importantly having their own human frailties that we all do. Keep in mind also that "the philosophy" is not here to judge, but rather to provide for the first time in the history of mankind, a rudimentary understanding of our true nature and purpose in this universe. A foundation which would be used as a substructure for all religions. A foundation intended to provide a substructure so strong that it will allow all religions to move into the forefront once again and to march next to man as a companion in his journey into the next millennia and into the heavens themselves. This should be a welcomed companion to man for the heavens are vast and will be a lonely place to be by ourselves. Religions cannot accompany us peacefully until they manage to find solace and tolerance with one another and within themselves. This will take a foundation upon which they must rest that does not yet exist, perhaps "the philosophy" can either provide or lead us to find just such a foundation.

With this in mind, let's look at Judas and see how an "evil" man may not be "evil" but quite the contrary; how he may be just a man like the rest of us. With this comes the possibility that the rest of us have hope for ourselves, that we may indeed be "good" people and that maybe there are a lot of "good" people in this world. With this comes the possibility that if we look within ourselves and do not like what we see, that we will realize that it is never too late to change. That in fact we have an obligation to other men's souls to make the necessary changes and then proceed to live out the rest of our lives in the quest to fulfill our purpose in this reality.

Let's look at Judas and see if we might be able to give this man, his soul, some peace. Let's see if we can see the "good" in him so that we may find "good" in ourselves and the rest of our fellow men with whom we often have little patience. Let's look at Judas through the eyes of western religion and then through the eyes of all religions, and add to these "the philosophy" to see how it would alter our perceptions and possible history.

Judas was one of the most visible "traitors" of the past two millennia. A man who, through a symbolic act of love, a kiss, set into motion the beginning of the last 2,000 years, the beginning of the age of A.D. itself. And just why is he supposedly so notorious, why has his very soul been so loathed by men, why has his soul over the last 2 millennia had to face the hate, disgust, and absolute despisement of the onslaught of millions of souls over the ages as they passed through his soul on their return to God?

The Christian institutions over the ages condemned Judas for betraying "their" God. They judge when they teach the concept to "judge not least ye be judged". They went against their own teachings. Why? It cannot be said for sure, but one thing is clear; it has served them well. It has helped to advance their traditions, institutions, and convictions. The judgment process has acted as just one more coalescent point around which their traditions have been able to rally.

But to what end has this occurred? It has occurred at the expense of a man's name, at the expense of a man's reputation, at the expense of a man's possible suffering in eternity as his soul has to face the negative emotions, through the ripple effect, suffered by other souls due to his actions. Emotions felt in life by souls as they agonized over their God's suffering caused by what they perceive to be the traitorous act of the man known as Judas.

What more symbolic way for Christ to begin His ordeal than through the symbolic act of love, the act of a kiss. And if Judas had not provided the act of a kiss, Christ would have had to find another way to begin His ordeal.

Judas made a mistake, as we perceive it, but that in itself is a judgmental statement and after all, if we follow the teachings of all religions, just who are we to be judgmental.

But assuming we are judgmental, and assuming we are correct, that does not mean he is condemned, through the ripple effect, to any more of a hell than the rest of us. In fact it could be quite the contrary, as will be seen, when viewing this episode through "the philosophy".

Christian religions, however, vilify the man because he betrayed "their" God. This was his sin in the eyes of the Church. But Judas was a man and Christ was considered to be a man, not God by men of his day and in fact is, even today, considered to be a man by most men of the world. Even Peter, his most ardent follower, denied him three times. So Judas identified him as a man, in the garden, and the Church has condemned him for it through the ages. The Church has used him over the millennia for their own purpose, as a tool around which to rally their following.

And did disciples console him with the teachings of Christ or did they let him agonize over his human actions, alone in the depths of despair? Were they there to console and comfort him as a fellow soul as he writhed in emotional agony through his short remaining days? Maybe they did not have the ability or opportunity to do so, but this we know; the Church has had, over the millennia, the opportunity to acknowledge Judas' humanness but has, for the most part, refused to do so.

How might this have been different had "the philosophy" been in place? (This is strictly theoretical since the information needed to develop this concept was not in existence at the time). Let's take a look at Judas through the eyes of "the philosophy". Judas was a man. Judas came from God Himself as a piece of God Himself. Judas was therefore, like the rest of us, like Christ Himself, God. Judas being human and his soul, God itself, existing in an amnesiac state apart from God, was not infallible, as again is the case of the rest of us.

We all take actions that hurt our fellow man and we all will feel its effects through the ripple effect. But Judas was a good man who took an action against someone that has affected history for more than two thousand years. His actions affected the souls of billions of other men throughout the millennia. Let's look at these two aspects, his actions against Christ, and then how his actions affected other men.

Judas' actions against Jesus was one action. One action against a very understanding and forgiving human. A man who was supposedly able to truly forgive other men for their actions against him.

If one is to face one's negative as well as positive actions through the ripple effect once having passed through this reality, then who would you rather have done harm to: men who have limited abilities to transcend negative actions taken against themselves or a man that has the unique ability to truly accept the shortcomings of men and forgive?

Once returning to the essence of the Creator of which he was a part in the first place, Judas' soul would feel the soul of Jesus flow through him. Would this be a cold soul or a soul of warmth and forgiveness? A soul that might have actually forgiven before the action took place. If this be the case, the soul of Christ as it passed through the soul of Judas in the hereafter, would have had little to impart unto Judas but love and forgiveness. Not a bad experience for Judas.

But then comes part two for Judas. To truly empathize with the souls of men as they returned to God to be a part of God again. Their very souls would probably be quite marked by the actions of Judas. The sorrow, despair, resentment, etc. that they felt would be quite intense and deep and Judas would most likely feel it all in the ripple effect.

This would be his hell. And who would have brought this on? Men. Some out of ignorance, some in an attempt to advance their own cause, some in an attempt to advance the cause of Christianity, some unable to follow the teachings of their own religion because they followed the teachings of men within their religion instead. Would Judas, then, be the only one to experience this ripple effect? No, for men, throughout the ages, regardless of their intent, who perpetuated the judgment of Judas in an erroneous manner, also have to face the ripple effects. A no win – no win situation for everyone.

In all cases, however, one thing stands out. All the actions were premised upon a lack of understanding of man. An understanding of where man came from, what his purpose is in life, what our purpose is as individuals, how we fit into the scheme of things, and just what is the purpose of it all.

Here is where "the philosophy", an understanding of who man is, an understanding of where man originated, an understanding of man and mans' purpose in reality, would have altered the course of history's perception of Judas.

As a foundation, "the philosophy" would have established that Judas was a piece of God Himself. It would have established that at the same time Judas was susceptible to the weakness of being both in an amnesiac state from God and being human. Lastly, "the philosophy" would have infused into men of his time that Judas, too, had a purpose in his life's journey.

Just as importantly, "the philosophy" would have made men realize that their actions or lack of actions towards Judas would be theirs to face throughout eternity through the ripple effect just as Judas would have to face the repercussions for his own actions.

Judas will have much company in any suffering he has to face and his companions in suffering will be men falsely judging him and using him for their own purpose.

With "the philosophy" established as a foundation, men would have had no choice but to approach Judas after his act in an entirely different fashion. They would have had no choice but to have comforted him, reminded him of his humanness, encouraged him to accept his frailties, and encouraged him to face the fact that he would be unable to change the past nor avoid facing the repercussions in the afterlife, all the while reminding him that he still had much of his journey, his quest, in this reality to complete to the best of his human limited abilities. And Judas had much to contribute to mankind at this point.

How might this have changed the course of history? First, Judas may not then have hanged himself in despair over the idea of looking into judgmental human eyes for the rest of his life. Rather, Judas would have known he would have the rest of his life to look into the eyes of men filled with love and acceptance. Second, Judas might then have spent the rest of his life preaching and spreading the concept of forgiveness regardless of the magnitude of the action. He surely would have acted as a excellent model for this. Thirdly, Judas would have been an excellent disciple of the concept of tolerance, which the Church has often lacked in its history not only in terms of external leadership but internal leadership for internal actions as well.

Change history, quite probably. An infusion of more tolerance, recognition that all men have a purpose and all men need encouragement, understanding, respect, and tolerance from their fellow men. This applies to, as well as needs to be extended from; the physically beautiful, talented, race and gender different, mentally retarded, disfigured, emotionally crippled, sexually different, and religiously unlike individuals.

"The philosophy" doesn't teach love. It doesn't teach compassion. It doesn't teach anything. What it does is truly revolutionary, but teaching is not a part of what it does. Religions do the teaching. Religions provide the guidelines. Religions are the homes for the weary souls as they make their journey through reality, as they take their leave temporarily from their true origins, god himself.

What does "the philosophy" do? It provides, for the first time, a foundation for religions, all religions. Before religious beliefs themselves were the foundation. It provides for the first time in the history of mankind, an understanding of where man comes from, who he is, what his soul is, what his purpose in this reality is, an understanding of how we can incorporate other intelligent life forms into our mindset, why we need to expand tolerance, why we need to listen to what religions have to say, why religions must stop trying to conform to each other and remain unique, and it goes on and on and on . . .

"The philosophy" explains why we must refocus our attitudes toward other men. When a philosophy can be broad enough to embrace Judas, a man condemned by the very religions that profess forgiveness itself, then perhaps it has some merit, perhaps it has enough uniqueness to deserve at least at elementary examination. And if it accomplishes this, and if this leads to a development of a more sophisticated philosophy than what we as men have in place today, one that builds upon, not destroys mans' past developments, then it will have been more successful than anything I could have imagined.

Perhaps the good of Judas as a life entity is to be expanded upon even more than his past unacknowledged contributions would have at first glance appeared to provide. Perhaps his existence, his suffering, had a purpose. The purpose of being a part of the realization of the need of a philosophy that can assist men, not destroy them. This then would surely expand upon the meaning of his life, the reason of the infusion of his very soul into this reality.

Likewise, if Judas, who has been condemned by the judgment of men for the last two thousand years, can have his value as a soul reexamined as to its importance, then surely you too can begin to accept that your life, your actions may not be as worthless as you sense or your fellow brothers may lead you to feel or believe.

It is time to give Judas some peace and what better time to start than at the beginning of a new millennia. How appropriate that the pieces of the puzzle to develop "the philosophy" should all finally surface and coalesce at this time.

Does man have a good side? There is no doubt. Sometimes we just have to look for it. Sometimes the individual has to implement it. Sometimes man and men need to look to the future, take heart and realize that they can implement the good and not give up in despair.

Good; if we can find it in Judas, we can find it all around us. Man unquestionably does have a good side.

Man's Good Side

We Are Our Brother's Keeper

"In Summary"

Judas Was A Man

Judas Was A Good Man

Men Use Other Men To Advance Their Own Causes

"The philosophy" Helps To Find The Good In All Men

"The philosophy" Acts As A Foundation To Religions

If Judas Has A Good Side, So Must All Men

It Is Time To Give Judas Some Peace

Go In Peace

"God does not look at your ledger figures or your wealth; he looks at your deeds."

Muhammad (570 – 632)
Prophet of Islam

Chapter 14:
Is It Worth It In The End?
♦
Is There Really A Heaven And A Hell?

Is there a "life" or consciousness after death? "The philosophy" is oriented around the concept that there is a life, a consciousness, after death since the reverse, no life or consciousness after death, has no meaning. Subsequently, the next logical question is, "If there is a life after death, is there a 'heaven' and a 'hell'?" Put into different words, the question might become, "Is the way I conduct my life today worth the energy I need to expend in order to conduct my life in a particular fashion?"

These are universal questions raised by mankind since the beginning of mans' recollections. And these questions lead logically to the universal questions that have haunted mankind such as: "**Is there hope for me as an individual?**", "Is there hope for mankind?", "**Religion – is it really significant or necessary?**", and "Is **omnipotence, omnipresence, and omniscience** really realistic or for that matter, logical?" These subsequent questions are extensive in nature and require some individual reflection. Therefore, they will be dealt with in the next four sections. For the present, however, let's focus in on "heaven and hell".

Since no life or consciousness after **death** makes everything, including this effort at writing a book or even your reading it, purposeless, we will proceed on the premise that "the philosophy" is correct, that there is a life or consciousness after death. This is not unique to "the philosophy". It has been proposed by every major religion and philosopher since the beginning of mankind.

Assuming that there is a life or consciousness after death, the next question is what is it like? Is there a **good** part to it and a **bad** part to it or in other words a heaven and a hell? According to "the philosophy" the answer would be yes with a capital "Y". Heaven and hell may not be quite what we imagined it to be, yet in actuality, it may be surprisingly more like what we had pictured than we could have possibly imagined.

One thing heaven and hell aren't is an intentional action on the part of the "Force" to punish or reward; rather it just is. If after experiencing life, one's being becomes one's actions (and not one's intentions) the "hell" is just that: the realization of the repercussions of one's actions to the rest of the "Force's" sensory devices. These beings or sensory devices (you and I in this case) have a purpose and negative actions (repressions, hostilities, acts of domination and violence), these acts of refusing to recognize the importance of each being in the scheme of things does nothing but interfere with the workings and success of the sensory device. This causes that being to react negatively to others in major or minor ways depending upon the severity of the actions. This becomes a Ripple Effect that moves through society and humanity. It does not stop with the one negative action but ripples through society.

After death, everyone is fully aware, conscious, of the effect of all their negative actions and not only the direct affect but all the infinite ripple effects the actions created as it undulates throughout humanity. Seeing is not the main Hell one will experience. Feeling and sensing in total the emotions and results of each action in all the possible manners will be a reality one will have to live with and continually experience for eternity. We will be a part of the Universal life force and thus able to sense in the true word all the emotions and pain we created in life and the pain and emotions this in turn created etc., etc. Depressing? No, not really, for the opposite is true also. We will sense in the truest of senses all the good we did and its Ripple Effect. All the good from the ambiguous little hello directed to the lonely individual we did not know was lonely to the direct actions of intentional helping hands that warmed the heart.

No, the good is not something that has to be awe-inspiring. It has but to warm the heart and boost the morale. It cannot be false for this leads to misconceptions by others regarding their being. Rather it must be honest (brutal honesty is not usually positive) and kind.

The violent man, the power hungry man, the users of others will in the end know in complete understanding and empathy the results of his actions to his fellow man. Everyone has some good, some more than others. The more one has, the less negative one has to feel and experience in the end. The more good one does, the more warmth one will experience in the next existence. Surely this is the meaning of, "You'll get yours in the end."

There will be no one to blame in the end. There will be no excuses. It will just "be". We are all able to make conscious decisions as to whether we will or whether we won't, regarding each action we take in life. We make that decision, not someone else. We are responsible for our own actions, for our own actions are our own actions and not someone else's.

If this is not enough to make men sit up and take note of what they are doing to each other, then that is too bad, for it is what it is and we will each live with the fact of our actions for eternity. Nothing will change the fact that we did what we did during our short physical lifetimes. And nobody can change the fact that we will live with it for eternity. This is not a punishment by God. We are a part of Him and will be again in the true merging sense. And what we take to Him will be our "contribution" and what we will exist with for eternity. Yes, it does make a difference what we do in life. No, we don't have to be "great" individuals for "greatness" is relative. As the saying goes, "If I cannot do great things, let me do little things in a great way." We have to learn and experience in life and remember we are becoming for an eternity what we created in actions and emotions. We are creating a live force of ourselves and we will truly "reap the fruits of our labors" in the end for eternity.

Does this mean we should try to rise above the tragedies of the moment? Absolutely. Does it mean we always can rise above these tragedies? Absolutely not! After all, in reality we do have to recognize that we are "just human". In the end, will we be able to hide behind the concept that we are "just human"? There will be no excuses. Remember? In the end it will just be. What was, was. What we did we did, and we will live with this forever into eternity and that's a long time.

There will be no intention to punish. It will just be what it is and that will be eternal awareness of literally everything we did, literally all the emotions it generated, throughout our lives, the lives of those in direct contact with us, how they in turn affected others due to our actions, and how those affected others, etc., etc.

Is there a heaven and a hell? I guess! ! ! What better way to live eternally than with the warmth of the true understanding and true empathy of the good we did and the good that in turn generated ad infinitum. On the other hand, what worse hell could be generated by sensing in every word imaginable of the total harm we administered upon our fellow man and the total effect it had on not only ourselves but upon other individuals in limiting the potential of what each had been able to bring back and contribute to the Omnipotence. What worse hell could be generated than being fully aware in every sense how one affected mankind in the negative regarding not only man's journey but man and mans' contribution to Omnipotence and mankind itself.

Is It Worth It In The End?

Is There A Heaven And A Hell?

"In Summary"

Significance Is Only Significant If It's Significant

1. No Eternal Life: Nothing Is Significant

2. Eternal Life: Everything Is Significant

If 1: Then There Is Literally Nothing To Worry About

If 2: Prepare For The Ripple Effect

God Is Omnipotent – He Does Not Need To Be Vindictive

Man Is His Own Worst Enemy

Man Is His Own Best Friend

Heaven Will Be Hell For All Of Us

"It is beneath human dignity to lose one's individuality and become a mere cog in the machine."

Mohandas K Gandhi
(1869 – 1948)

Chapter 15:
Is There Hope For You As An Individual?
♦
Hope Is All We Have

Is there hope for you? Is there hope for the individual? Of course. All religions profess it. "The philosophy" is not a religion, just a foundation for man, a foundation for religions. As a crude universal philosophy, "the philosophy" reinforces the concepts of hope put forward through the ages by religions, deja vu, and universal mythologies. The concept of hope for the individual is a concept that science and philosophy have been attempting to rationalize since their formation.

Is there hope for everyone? Certainly, everyone has done some good at some point. The total sum of constructive actions and their ripple effect may not outweigh the total sum of the destructive actions and their ripple effect, but everyone will experience some positive.

Be careful, however, for you are responsible for your actions. Asking for forgiveness may lead to forgiveness but you are still responsible and using excuses will not absolve you of the repercussions that will follow you into eternity from the after-effects of your action within this reality.

Receiving forgiveness from the creator as a whole entity is

one thing, but even the whole entity cannot protect you from what was and what was is in fact the influence you had or could have had on specific individuals. A wrong committed through action or inaction involves three entities: the individual in this reality, society – the whole of individuals in this society, and the whole of the creative force for whose purpose we are here and of which we are literally a part. Forgiveness received from the whole may absolve one of the wrath of the whole in our reinfusion back into God, which granted is by no means trivial, but it still leaves the trauma and warmth of our experiencing the effects of our influence from this reality of the individuals we affected within this reality.

Even the whole will not be able to prevent you from "reaping what you have sown". It will not be a punishment, just a realization of what you have, in every sense of the word, wrought upon your fellow man within this reality. Once returning to God, being God yourself, you will have full knowledge of what others have done and what you have done. Everyone will have some shame, some more than others. Everyone will have glory, some more than others.

Saying you did not know, did not understand, or wouldn't have done what you did if you had only known, will not change the fact that you will be fully aware of the effects of your actions and experience them for yourself, not as punishment, just as a case of "that's what happens". Think about what you do and do not take it lightly.

Let's take an example of some typical people and, attempting to be nonjudgmental, let's examine their actions according to "the philosophy" in order to get a sense of how one might view one's own actions using the additional insights "the philosophy" provides.

The Impact 171

An interesting segment of society to look at is the immense new segment of society: the informational sector. This sector has grown phenomenally in scope in the last one hundred years. It now enters the homes of almost everyone worldwide. It influences and molds developing generations. It sets the tone of the individual's day. It provides a mindset regarding how everyone views their fellow man and how they actually interact with them. The seeds of the mindset for the individual may be planted as seeds of caution, suspicion, bigotry, intolerance, impatience, and fear or the seeds of the mindset for the individual may be planted as seeds of warmth, trust, cooperation, understanding, respect, connection.

This media is practically everywhere in our present civilization. It sweeps through our lives by means of newspapers, magazines, radio, TV, movies, computer networks, billboards, song lyrics, slogans on clothing, plays, books, and art itself. It is almost an omnipresence in itself. One finds it almost impossible to get away from. It has become an integral part of our life process. Being so large, it requires a vast array of individual souls to perpetuate it, distribute it, create it, and preserve it. Since it is a creation of souls, and cannot exist without souls, its function, purpose, and direction will continue to be dependent upon men's souls.

With no understanding of one's purpose in life, the messages displayed by this sector has a lack of purpose and direction. It goes wherever the momentum carries it and the momentum is never analyzed as to a direction since no purpose is established by which to gauge direction. With no understanding of where one came from before entering this reality, the souls working within the sector of the informational media have no sense of their roots. With no sense of their roots, the souls of the creators of the messages, portrayed through the informational sector, have no sense of what messages they wish to dedicate themselves. The messages, therefore, become conflicting, chaotic, contradicting as a whole and wears away at the souls it reaches.

With no understanding of how the results of one's actions in life will impact one's soul, the individuals, dedicating a major portion of their waking hours to the creation of messages with which they wish to bombard fellow souls, have no sense of responsibility to other souls. They have no sense of responsibility to themselves, their very souls, their very own eternity.

This sector in society has grown phenomenally in a short period of time. It has refined its process of putting out messages it wants heard in such convincing words, techniques, suggestions, and frequency that whatever message is presented the most, becomes almost a situation of intentional brainwashing of large numbers of individuals. Of course, the informational sector would deny this. It is counterproductive for them to admit the power of their techniques but just ask the millions of organizations that pay to have their messages displayed.

Of course the public will deny the brainwashing concept. No one wants to think they are "dumb" enough to accept any truth to soap operas, to the sexual messages of aftershave commercials, or to the message of rape being what every woman wants as is verbalized in today's modern music. But it's there and much much more. It's found in society in music, books, magazines, movies. It's on billboards, tee shirts, container labels, TV screens. It's shot through the air into our radios in our cars, walkmans, buses, places of work, recreation facilities, dining halls, and even the schools in which we send our children.

The strength of the messages are minute in their singularity but enormous in their multiplicity. They inundate the auditory and visual senses of men minute after minute, hour after hour, day after day, week after week, year after year. Is it any wonder that men are becoming unprincipled, intolerant, and impatient?

Many messages are produced by souls with no thought as to how their work influences other souls, influences society as a whole, influences the very journey of souls. The negative messages are produced in a vacuum, by souls with no conviction. Produced by souls with no sense of an understanding of their foundation. Produced by souls, themselves lost, in the vast sea of incessant flashing messages surrounding and washing through them.

Are we to set standards as to what can and cannot be produced? That has to be done by the individual within himself. The individual needs to say to himself, "Is this message I am creating, producing, working to broadcast, or financing what I want my fellow souls, men, to do, think, understand, believe, follow, and act upon? Will my actions be helpful to myself and others?"

Religions provide some direction for these decisions, but man is moving past using only the religious explanation of "do it because you have faith". Man still feels the comfort of the house of religion. Man still feels the subconscious drive to follow the religious beacons. But man also senses that something is missing and is impatient for its exposure. Man is missing the answer to questions such as: "Why?", "Who am I?", "What is my purpose in life?", "Where did I come from?", "Where will I be going after life?"

What does this have to do with the information segment of society and the individual's actions within this sector? Almost everything. Presently, the information sector is awash with introspection as well as public scrutiny. It is filled with chaos, lack of direction, lack of comprehensive purpose, and uncertainty of its own merits and influence.

Influence it has, while influence it denies for fear of losing it. Its believers spend hundreds and hundreds of billions of dollars annually in its productions and distributions. If there were any uncertainty at all as to its effectiveness, this would not be the case.

"The philosophy" then enters the picture through its explicit explanation of how each person, individually functioning as a part of the informational sector, has a responsibility to himself, other souls, and the whole of God to which he will return. His responsibility lies in the end product and the effect that product has in relationship to the journey of souls and to the journey of his own soul.

Don't misunderstand, the process described does not apply to just the informational sector. It applies to all individuals and to all sectors of society in which individuals participate. Each action taken by each person involved needs to be preceded by the question: Is this beneficial to society? Do I want to be part of the final effect this product will have upon souls journeying through my time frame?

Granted these are judgmental questions. But since each individual will have to live with the results of his actions through eternity, they not only have the right to ask but the responsibility to their own souls to ask if they want to be a part of the actions taking place. A universal philosophy will be one that elevates responsibility and places it squarely upon the individual taking the actions. The days of a leader drumming out messages of bigotry and hatred followed by the annihilation of fifty million people in the course of six long years are hopefully over. The day of a few thousand people in black boots and smart uniforms saying, "I was just following orders", is hopefully over.

Hopefully, a universal philosophy will help provide an understanding of our purpose as individuals in this reality. An understanding that will add strength to mankind's foundations of religion, which in turn will revitalize man's recognition of the importance of his responsibilities, the importance of his journey within this cosmos.

Hopefully . . . hopefully . . . hopefully . . . If there is no hope for the individual, there is no hope.

Hope is all we have.

Hope For You As An Individual?

Hope Is All We Have

"In Summary"

There Is Hope For Everyone

Forgiveness Doesn't Absolve Responsibility

Negative Actions Have Three Negative Effects

Positive Actions Have Three Positive Effects

The Impact Of The Informational Media Is Phenomenal

A Singular Message Has Little Impact

A Multiplicity Of Singular Messages Adds Up To Major Impact

You Are Responsible For Your Actions

"I Was Just Following Orders" Won't Cut It

"There are two ways of exerting one's strength: one is pushing down, the other is pulling up."

Booker T. Washington
American educator
(1856 – 1915)

Chapter 16:
Is There Hope For Mankind?
♦
And The Swirling Waters Of The Lack Of Convictions Continue Their Process Of Eroding Away The Pillars

Our hands reach out and immerse themselves in the heavens. Reality, not one but many. They are as the stars in the sky, seemingly finite but apparently infinite. And during the day they seem not to exist; but during the nights, in the quiet, in the warmth of the summer's darkness that surrounds man, they pop out like little jewels on black velvet. In the serenity of isolation we examine them, wonder over them, and dream of someday being there. And the void continues to reveal itself to us, entice us, draw us in.

First we knew of one, our own. Now we consider four, **Bega**. Tomorrow we will dream of a sky full of them and draw together, huddle together as men, as mankind, exposed to the humbling understanding of our true place in the scheme of things. Huddle we will for our self-centeredness as man and men, our visions of righteousness and grandeur of ourselves and our species will pale and become lost as the night sky begins to unfold and the multitude of stars begin to display their elegance. And we will stand in awe.

Despair in our insignificance? We will have little time to do so for the magnitude of our purpose will cause us to understand that we either stand shoulder to shoulder with each other and stand tall or we shall fade away as a dying star.

We control our destiny. We control our accomplishments. We control the magnitude of our contribution to the Omnipotence, the Omniscience, the Omnipresence that created our reality, that created the myriad of realities that stretch out before us hidden by the darkness of vast distance.

We, each and everyone of us, must no longer stand alone. We, each and everyone of us, must draw together shoulder to shoulder; stand tall and proud in the awe of our purpose and, joining hands, together must reach for the stars as individuals working in conjunction with the whole, separate but united, our feet rooted in the earth of our reality.

And the void surrounds us. And while our hands reach out and immerse themselves in the heavens awash with the wonders of the undiscovered, our feet are rooted in the understanding of our reality. And we begin to see, that both what is above and what is below, are connected in the far distance by a soft wall of a Creator. A warm, glowing force of which we are a part. A force so alive it quivers with anticipation of what it is to learn. And we as individuals, as a species, are a part of the reason it shimmers and shakes, for we, as man and men, are also a means for it to eek out new knowledge, new experiences, new creations. We are a means of the growth of its very omniscience, omnipotence, and omnipresence. And it trembles in anticipation of what we have to bring it, to bring ourselves, for He is us and we are He.

And so the void is and we temporally are a part of it, with our hands immersed in the heavens of discovery and our feet rooted in reality. And there we stand as stalagtites and stalagmites in the caverns of the void. And so it is with souls. Some journey with their hand immersed in the heavens touching God but their feet dangling above the floor of reality; other souls stand tall with their feet embedded in the floor of reality and their hands reaching up but not quite being able to reach God. Both magnificent in their convictions and faiths. Then comes those which grow with their feet rooted in reality and their hands immersed in the wonders of the heavens.

There we stand, our feet rooted to God and our hands extended upward touching God. There we stand, as God, finally realizing the reality of it all. And so goes a universal philosophy. And so goes a crude attempt at a universal philosophy through quadratics, through "the philosophy."

And so it goes. The pillars of society continue to hold up the roof of order over civilization, standing on the foundation of religion, of knowledge, of universal mythology, of philosophy, of deja vu, of faith. And the pillars provide the support which in turn allows for the continuation of men's souls to seek to accomplish their journey's purpose as they peer into the outer regions of the darkness of the void and light up bits and pieces of it through their curiosity and rationality. And so it reveals itself.

Other men examine the details of the exposed void and find order in seemingly endless lack of order. They find beauty in the simplicity of the sparkling crystals of creation impregnated in the pillars, heavens, and foundation of the void within which we find ourselves.

The pillars stand as towers of strength. They are composed of the greats: Ghandi, Aristotle, Mohammed, Luther, Gutenberg, Moses, Plato, Shakespeare, Mozart, Picasso, Nobel, Confucius, Churchill, Beethoven, da Vinci, Dante, Nostradamus, Rembrant, T'ao Ch'ien, Christ, and the pillars go on and on and spread out from a location within our void to the very edge of the darkness which has yet to be rolled back by man and men.

Some of the pillars are clearly labeled and strong as time itself, composed of truth, beauty, uniqueness, and reality itself. Their light radiates through the darkness of the void and acts as sources of warmth, strength, and solace around which men gather, contemplate, regenerate themselves, and work.

Some of the pillars are less prominent but vital nonetheless in their function as pillars. Their names may not be clearly etched but their contributions, their lights, radiate throughout the void. Then come the common pillars, strong in their conviction, resolute in their principles, determined in their drive to stand firm against the weight of oppression of men and the cracking of the foundations of faith. These are common pillars. These are the little recognized pillars. These are the crux of the support system that hold up the roof of civilization. These pillars are you, your neighbors, fathers, mothers, doctors, lawyers, custodians, engineers, sanitation workers, scientists, teachers, brothers, sisters, waitresses, cooks, big people, little people, and on and on and on. All of vital importance.

And new pillars are being built all the time. And new pillars are developing their strength, their knowledge, their convictions and principles in order to stand with the pillars that stand today. These are the children. Well we should look after them, well we should nurture them, well we should train them and prepare them for they are the future. They will be the ones to face the challenge of their own journeys, sometimes alone, sometimes with companions. They will be the ones to carry on mankind's search to accomplish its purpose.

And as the void reveals itself in the light and expands, we begin to see the waters. The rivers and oceans of knowledge, creativity, and beauty begin to emerge. So too does the flood of hate, jealousy, greed, pity begin to overflow the banks and swirl around the pillars, incessantly eroding away at their base.

So it goes and history continues to repeat itself. Many are the times the roof has given way. Many are the times the roof has collapsed only to have to be rebuilt again by others. The roof never collapses due to its own lack of importance. It always collapses due to the eroding away of the very pillars that hold it up in the first place. An erosion process with the force of water. Water mixed with the abrasive grains of pettiness, envy, jealousy, lack of purpose, greed, lack of self control, dishonesty to oneself as well as others, belittlement of the concept of individual responsibility for one's own actions, and the list goes on and on.

Many are the pillars that are needed to support the roof above us. The more advanced we become as a species, the more crowded our globe gets, the more pillars that are needed to support the roof above us. Civilizations need a roof of social order over them. For some civilizations the roof was more grand than others.

Regardless of how grand the roof of civilization appeared, the roof was supported by pillars of society made up of the "common" man. Mothers, fathers, teachers, religious leaders, government officials, law enforcement officials, tradesmen, educated, uneducated, skilled, unskilled – the list is too numerous to complete.

Each soul in its own way contributing to support the roof not only above themselves but above others as well. Each soul forming a pillar in their own right, yet as wires being wound around each other to form cable, working together to form a pillar of importance such as a family unit, an educational institution, a medical facility, a monetary institution to mention but a few.

What often happens in history, however, is that the waters of uncertainty made up of the lack of belief in one's importance in the scheme of things and begins to wear away at the pillars in society. As some erode away, they add to the abrasiveness of the waters surrounding the remaining pillars which in turn begin to erode away. This is countered by the continual building of new pillars by the family unit.

The process of erosion and building are not ever in equilibrium. History has shown us many instances of the collapse of the social order, the roof above us. In fact throughout mans' history, never once have we seen a roof remain forever intact. The Greeks, Aztecs, Egyptians, Romans, Chinese, Europeans, Americans, to name just a few, have all had their roofs collapse.

Each time, however, the roof is rebuilt and in fact seems to grow in size. Its location changes, its language changes, but its ultimate drive always seems to be pointed in the same direction– discovery, expansion, creativity.

Will our present roof collapse again? Who knows. Maybe not, for once. Maybe we have finally reached a turning point in mankind's history. Many unique situations have culminated at this point in time; instantaneous global communications, global communities, the turn of the millennium, global recognition of the brotherhood of men, and the importance of the individual. True, the concepts have not gained full maturity yet, but the seeds have been planted globally.

Never before have we reached a point in history when the destiny of a few, such as at Kent State and Tienenman Square, was able to shame total nations immediately and unforgivingly. Never before have we been at the edge of literally jumping to the stars, a task so immense it will take the willpower, cooperation, and commitment of all men working together.

With a little more support added to our present foundations, a universal philosophy, perhaps our foundations, will support our dreams. Perhaps, at this point in time, things will be different.

Is there hope for mankind? Absolutely! Is our time at hand? Perhaps . . .

That is up to us . . . all of us.

Hope for Mankind?

Lack Of Conviction Erodes Away The Pillars

"In Summary"

Hands Stretched Upward Towards The Dream Of The Stars

Feet Planted In Reality

Man Rolls Back The Darkness Of The Void

Man, Men, Stretched Upward, Form Pillars

Pillars Support the Roof of Order

The Roof Has Always Collapsed

The Rebuilding Process Goes On Continually

We Need More Support To Our Foundations

This Time Things Will Be Different, Perhaps . . .

"Religion is a candle inside a multicolored lantern. Everyone looks through a particular color, but the candle is always there."

Mohammed Naguib (b. 1901)
Egyptian soldier and politician

Chapter 17:
Religion Is It: Significant/Necessary? Which One?

♦

Man Has No Faith In Religion

What myths we burden our children with in order to scare them into behavior we wish to perpetuate: "God is watching you." "God will punish you for that." "God doesn't approve of that."

These myths do nothing but instill deeply ingrained, intellectually stifling emotions regarding religion, philosophy, and tolerance permanently within the minds of our very own children. Fear is contagious and the young learn early and remember long. Why do we do this? What better way to honor thy father and mother than to listen to, retain, and then pass onto one's children the superstitions and myths which our very parents bestowed upon us? What better way for global religious organizations to perpetuate the continuation of their worldwide power and influence?

What other way existed for individual men and religious organizations to cover up their insecurity created by their lack of understanding of, knowledge of, let alone confidence in their purpose in the total scheme of reality? This lack of understanding by man, men, and religious institutions regarding their purpose in reality leads them all to overcompensate in their attempts to persuade others of their superior insights and traditions through the processes of intimidation, intolerance, coercion, guilt, rejection of cultural traditions, and fear. This they do in the "name of peace", for the "good of others", to "save all men", and "in the name of God, Himself". In actuality, we know they do it for the selfish reason of hoping to save their own souls.

Even as adults, we find it almost impossible, if not impossible, to shed the superstitions and religious insecurities ingrained into us by our parents and religions. Were our parents "bad" to do this? No, they just followed the way of their parents, their parent's parents, their parent's parent's parents, etc. It was a means to keep us in our "dens" and following guidelines and truths through the implementation of fear, while we grew and matured. It didn't keep us from poking our heads out of the den and gazing into the open heavens as we stared with awe and wonder at the whole universe stretching out above us, and beckoning us to venture into it. Rather than dampen our desires to romp in the wonders of the heavens, the containment shackles placed upon us by insufficient knowledge; poorly thought out, religiously imposed priorities; and self-serving desires of some men to dominate and control others; just intensified our desire to reach for that which we could not have. Now we can have it. Now we can have it all. Now we can step into the heavens.

To get what we have always wanted, to get what we have always dreamed of, will require us to alter the patterns of our parents. It will require us to set aside myths and move onto logic and reason. We are about to step into the heavens and we

The Impact 191

cannot encourage our children to do that while at the same time chaining them to superstitions and intellectually stunting fears perpetuated by religion, myths, and bigotry.

We must begin to use our religions as guides rather than shackles for our children. We must begin to use our religions as homes for the soul rather than as tools of suppression, guilt, and power. We must begin to have faith itself in religion and not fear the demise of religion through the recognition of its true purpose for man and men.

How do we get men freed up to stroll the heavens? How do we unlock the shackles that bind religions just as religions bind men? We start by answering the questions men have asked for eons. We start by defining man's and mans' purpose in life. We cannot do this alone. We must have religions participating and this will not happen until religion itself answers its need for a purpose within reality. Religion needs more than just a purpose centered around the glorification of God. Religion needs a real purpose in reality. Religion needs to find its own niche in reality or it will never concede to allowing man to establish his purpose in the universe.

Glorification is nice but it has no function other than to assume it is paying homage to a force that supposedly knows it is all knowing, omniscient (since it is all knowing it certainly doesn't need to be told that); all powerful, omnipotent (since it's all powerful and knows it, it surely doesn't need to prove it by implementing a policy that its creations better honor it or else); and all present. Even so, we persist in creating paradoxes relegating the creator of a universe to the limitations of humans. We persist in holding onto the myth that we can impose upon the creator of a universe, the reality in which we function, the stymieing characteristics of omnipotence, omniscience, and omnipresence using the reasoning that these three terms actually give the creator of the universe limitless qualities.

As contradictory as it may seem, the fact is that by describing the creator as omnipotence, omniscience, and omnipresence, we have actually done an injustice to the creator itself. We have stymied it to an existence of limitations. The limitations of the set of limits of: being everywhere already; knowing everything already; and being powerless to expand its own presence, knowledge, or power.

Placing these parameters on God makes our God too small. If there is a limit to everything, even God, it means we have a limit. It means there is no purpose for man in life but to glorify an egotistical force. It means there is no purpose in life for mankind but to try to reinforce the perception of an omnipotent, omniscient, and omnipresent being that it is in fact omnipotence, omniscience, and omnipresence, which it already knows. If that isn't a contradiction, what is?

How demoralizing, how demeaning, how restrictive the idea is that our only purpose in life is to glorify an omnipotence, omniscience, and omnipresence force that already knows it is just that. How senseless. No wonder we haven't reached a universal understanding of our fellow man. No wonder we haven't solved most of our social, economic, and moral problems.

We must expand our concept of life. We must begin to not just ask the question, "Why, what is my purpose in life? What is mans' purpose in life?" We must start to answer these questions, for the answers will free us of our shackles, which hold us to the security of this planet. The answers will lead us to looking at our fellow man in an entirely different light. It will force us to accept the concept that all men are equal; that all men have a purpose; that all men must aid others in the quest to fulfill their purpose in life for we will all benefit equally from the success of each man, each soul, in fulfilling that quest. The answers will illuminate the very paths we are trying to follow in the darkness of the night. The darkness of ignorance regarding our purpose in reality will then no longer obscure our paths.

We will never find our purpose as long we keep placing limits upon the creator of the universe itself, as long as we persist upon keeping our God small. How can we bestow upon the creator any greater characteristics than being omnipotent, omniscient, and omnipresent? By adding the dimension of recognizing that while this may be true, it does not mean that the creator of this universe is incapable of expanding its limits through increasing knowledge with knowledge that does not exist yet, expanding limits of its existence with space that does not exist yet, and augmenting power through the creation of new, not yet existing, knowledge and space.

That is what is called expanding the limits of a creator. What is really exciting is that we, man the machine – body and mind, then become its tools to do so. We, man the machine, then rise to a level of equality not only amongst each other as humans but also in regards to our relationship to other intelligent life forms that we might also find searching the heavens.

This concept of equality amongst ourselves and other intelligent life forms is also too limiting. This general concept is not acceptable in the eyes of the intuitive man nor in the eyes of religion, man's companion throughout life. We will never accept the concept that we are a machine and well we shouldn't. We are not the machine. We are really the soul, God Himself, and the soul uses the machine, man, as its vehicle of travel as it seeks out accomplishing its purpose in life. The soul eeks out bits and pieces of new knowledge to bring back to the creator of the universe. Each man is indispensable. Each man has a purpose. Each individual man may not find the actual bits and pieces himself; but each man in his own specific manner aids other men in doing so. The knowledge is not easily gleaned and we don't even know where to find it, but we will find it. The effort needed to find it is immense and takes the cooperative effort of all men. We must all join in the effort. We must all work together. We must recognize that each of us, no matter who he is, has a role to play, and that each role is of equal importance.

We are like children afraid to venture out of the nest. We know the whole universe is out there to explore but we are too timid to do more than peek our heads out of the den. We are too timid to take our first serious step into space. It has been twenty-five years since the first moon walk and we haven't been anywhere since. We made our first step and then we withdrew like timid cubs.

It took us only ten years to get to the moon once we set our minds to it as a team of men. It was our first step into the heavens. Since then, we have used every excuse under the sun to stay in the security of our present surroundings. It's too expensive; so was the project of lacing our country from ocean to ocean with ribbons of superhighways. It's too dangerous; so was sailing the Atlantic in 1492. Someone may die; people die driving cars, flying in planes, and eating food. The space shuttle explodes; so did a chemical plant in New York. We have diseases to fight, crime to attend to, and poverty to eliminate; we always have had and we probably always will have these elements with which to contend.

Why the excuses? Why the hesitation? Our curiosity regarding the heavens has always been with us since the beginning of recorded time. Why the deliberate diversion of our energies to reach out and grab hold of our very destiny as men, our destiny of soaring into the heavens? Our purpose of seeking out and also of actually creating new knowledge.

How ironic that we, using God's name, shackle ourselves, as a species, to this earth. We act like children blaming their parents for their lack of courage to try new and exciting ventures. We do it with petty human vindictiveness as we bestow, as adults no less, the humanness of limits upon the creator of our universe which represents the very reality in which we function. We do it with primitive myths perpetuated with statements and questions such as "How could God do that to me?" "Why do good people suffer?" "God decided his time was up." "Its God's way of saying no." "Its God's way of punishing them." "Because that's what God wants."

We withdraw into our den of security, find excuses for not venturing out of our dens, and at the same time snatch peeks of the heavens above as we romp in our confined den attempting to impinge individual dominance upon those who share the space of the den with us.

We stay within our den believing we are safe, not thinking about the fact that as we grow older we are going to grow bigger, and as we grow bigger we are going to become crowded within the confines of the very home which has provided us the security we needed. Eventually contamination, disease, social violence, or just plain boredom will prove to be our doom.

Man will have the same problem as mice have when confined in a utopian environment. Under these conditions, mice began to just die. Not from lack of food, disease, violence, or genetic factors, they just lose the will to live. They lose their need to struggle to survive, they lose their purpose to live.

Men need a purpose in life. Mankind needs a purpose to survive. The purpose cannot, however, be something we want it to be. It has to be what it is or what it most logically seems to be when considering the information we have culled through intuition, religion, science, and philosophy. It has to make sense and it has to transcend all four yet embrace all four because intuition, religion, science, and philosophy have been the cornerstone of mans' search for his purpose in the total scheme of things.

Is religion significant and necessary? Absolutely, it is one of the four cornerstones of man. Which one? Whichever is of comfort to one's soul. Whichever one will best aid your soul in its journey through its present life form, its present reality.

Religion
Significant / Necessary?

"In Summary"

Our God Is Too Small!

Man Has No Faith In Religion

If A Force Is Omnipotent, Omniscient, And Omnipresent,
It Does Not Need To Be Constantly Told So

Omnipotence, Omniscience, Omnipresence
Is Too Restrictive For God

You Are God, I Am God, That's Why We:

1. Are Brothers
2. Are All Indispensable
3. Have A Common Purpose
4. Need To Step Off This Good Earth

Religions Also Have A Purpose

> *"Take, for instance, a twig and pillar, or the ugly person and the great beauty, and all the strange and monstrous transformations. These are all levelled together by Tao. Division is the same as creation; creation is the same as destruction."*
>
> Chuang-tzu (369 – 286 B.C.)
> *On Leveling All Things*

In Summary: The Soul

♦

Who Man Really Is

Female, male, black, yellow, white, dumb, ugly, beautiful, handicapped, talented, adult, child, old, young? There are no such things. They are all concepts and perceptions created by individuals to further their life ambitions to dominate others. Misnomers created by men using the facade of culture to subjugate their own fellow men in order to advance their own agendas within this life frame. Twisted misconceptions intentionally interjected into religious thought by short-sighted men intent upon gaining "power" and "superiority" over others. Men so possessed by their obsession to "advance themselves" that they stoop to the level of actually contaminating religion, the shelter for the traveling soul, to the extent of twisting religion and religious concepts into perverted tools. Tools which they hope will assist them in their obsession to advance their own power and influence at the expense of others.

Why the problems? Why the racism? Why the gender wars? Why the intolerance? Why the power plays? The questions can go on and on and on. The reason is really quite simple. Man has not defined who he is or what his purpose is in this reality. Man has not had, until this point, a sufficient amount of religious, deja vu, and scientific data to allow himself to hypothesize a logical reason for his existence. A logical understanding of who he really is.

Without this understanding and acceptance of purpose, without this realization and acceptance of who he is, man and man-made institutions will do nothing but continue their course of subjecting others in order to establish themselves as individuals and organizations of supposed superior influence and importance. Man and institutions will continue to perpetuate the misconceptions of their individual importance over others rather than see others as their equals. Man and institutions will continue to sacrifice their fellow brothers for the benefit of their own gain. How short-sighted, for our individual travels within this reality are but a flicker of a candle in the hourglass of time.

Does man now have a sufficient amount of religious, deja vu, and scientific data to allow himself to hypothesize a logical reason for this existence? A logical understanding of who he really is? Possibly. Part I of this book attempts to coalesce just such information and if it is not a sufficient beginning, then man must find the answer. For the answer to mans' and man's purpose and who he is, is the only universal glue that will allow man to step above all the intolerance that has plagued him throughout history.

Once man realizes that his body is not who he is, man will gain a different perspective regarding others. Religions have brought us a long way in regards to this very fact. What they have lacked, or maybe been afraid of defining, is an acceptance of a man's purpose in this reality. Lacked, because they are reluctant to accept science as a coequal in mans' search for purpose. Feared, because, with the recognition of mans' purpose in reality, religion's role will change and no one, including institutions, like change. Feared because, with change, may come a radically new role which will no longer include the ability of religions to dominate, subjugate, or intimidate man and men.

Just what concept could be so significant as to intimidate and threaten the most powerful, influential, and dominating men and institutions of our time or time to come?

The simple concept that Man is not man the machine, and who we are as individuals, is not man himself, but rather the soul is who we are as individuals. Religions have been saying this forever, it seems, true, but religions have not grasped the purpose of the soul. They have professed man and mans' purpose to be the glorification of God as described in "**Religion: Significant/Necessary? Which One?**" Religions have not allowed man to see that his purpose is to expand upon the omniscience, omnipresence, and omnipotence of the creator Himself. That we, ourselves, individually, are here to do that very thing. That we, our souls, are actually all one with other souls (and although temporarily fragmented from each other), will in the end, blend back into one. That we, our souls, are actually all equal in brotherhood and equal in purpose. That it is we, our souls, that were created in the image of God, not our bodies and minds. That we, our souls, are actually God Himself, ourselves.

The only difference between us is that we, our souls, were placed into different vessels, machines, bodies. Each of us must learn to cope with the limitations of the machine in which we were placed. Limitations of: size, intellectual ability, appearance, physical ability, neurology, hormones, organ imperfections, etc., etc.

Our bodies and minds are amazing tools with amazing abilities, but they each have their own special limits. The soul occupying a particular mind and body must maximize the potential of that very mind and body in order to maximize its own success at fulfilling its purpose in this reality.

We must each support other souls for they also have the same goal as we. They will bring back to God, to ourselves, what they have learned in order to expand upon the omniscience, omnipresence, and omnipotence of not just the creator but of, in actuality, oneself and every other soul.

How would the concept, of man being God Himself, change the status and role of the powerful, influential, and dominating individuals in society? It would truly equalize all men. Not equalize them in words, but in the very purpose of life itself. It would raise the status of the homeless to the status of the corporate executive. It would raise the status of the interrogated to the status of the despot. It would raise the status of the common man to the status of royalty.

How would, the concept of man being God Himself, change the status and role of religion, the most powerful and influential institution created by man (not God). It would reverse the role of man and religion. No longer would man be secondary to religion and thus be at the bidding of religion. Now religion would be secondary to man and thus be at the bidding of man. For man would be recognized as God Himself.

How significant! How revolutionizing! No longer would any

man be subjected to degradation, intimidation, torture, abuse, intolerance, subjugation, and indifference. For as individual men and institutions attempted or succeeded to abuse their fellow men, they would have to accept that in fact they were abusing God Himself. They would have to accept that in fact they were abusing, in actuality, their very selves. No longer could men accept the orders of the powerful as an acceptable excuse to aide others for there will be no rationalizing away one's actions, one's abuse of God Himself. We will all live with the repercussions of our actions through the ripple effect for eternity.

It would be the soul, God Himself, that individual men and institutions would be interfering with in terms of God's very own quest to expand upon His very own omniscience, omnipresence, and omnipotence. And as men and religions of power and influence have been professing forever, have continually impressed upon the "common man", "You do not want to get in the way of God!"

"In Summary"

**Man's Lack of Understanding:
Of Who He Is And What His Purpose Is
Leads To Intolerance**

**Men and Institutions Subjugate Their Fellow
Men Because Of Ignorance**

The Body And Mind Are Not Man

The Soul Is Man

All Men Are Truly Equal

**Religion And Powerful Men Are Afraid
Of The Truth**

The Truth WILL Set Us Free

We Are Each God

God Wants Man To Be Independent

The Ripple Effect Returns

Part B.

Man's

Society

The Present

B. MAN'S SOCIETY/THE PRESENT
Social Dilemmas are not Dilemmas............206

Introduction
The Crumbling Foundation............209

19. Status
  Social/Occupational/Economic Illusions, Perpetuated by the Ones it Hurts Most...221

20. Atheism/Religion
  The Atheist has a Soul, He too is God, But yet a Lonely Place He Occupies............231

21. War/Abortion
  Take Care of your own Soul............239

22. Suicide
  So you don't Feel so Good?............251

23. Death Penalty/Life Incarceration
  A "Debt to Society" is a Debt Owed to Other Souls, It Can Never be Repaid............259

24. Letting Go/Forgiving
  You do not Need to Punish Men – They will Bring on their Own Punishment – Move on With Your Life............271

25. Missionary Work/Helping Others
  Everybody is a Missionary, Like it or Not............281

26. In Summary
  Intolerance is an Outmoded Term............293

Introduction:
The Crumbling Foundation
♦
The Present Is But A Fleeting Moment
The Future Will Inevitably Arrive

Societies build upon foundations that provide the bases for growth and advancement, but most of these foundations are rigid and unable to grow with society, thus leading to the collapse of the very society the foundation was able to germinate.

Each civilization builds upon the past. Each incorporates mans' basic convictions, deja vus, of the existence of a higher order. Each takes the advancement of the souls before them and rebuilds the collapsed structures with new and more magnificent civilizations, only to find themselves unable to reinforce the basic foundations upon which they were built. Thus each faces the inevitability of their own demise as a part of their future, the future that faced all civilizations before.

The total process is built upon the basic premise that intelligent life, man, was the unique creation of the gods or of God. All civilizations clutching to the hope, the belief, that man was so unique that only man was to transcend death. Man and his ability to reason, moves through history searching the heavens and digging deep within himself.

Man left no stone unturned except those too big to move. He used the tool of faith to carry him forward as he confronted trauma, despair, turmoil, and personal shortcomings. He never faltered, he always had hope and, despite the severity of any falls, he used hope to stand upon as he continued to rebuild each new civilization more beautiful than the last. Each holding the value of the individual higher and higher in its convictions that life was not life but rather just a temporary relocation of the soul, the essence of man.

As history moved on, so did man. His knowledge grew and his faith strengthened as he improved upon his lot from civilization to civilization as time moved forward. Before the fall of each civilization, each generation searched for means of reinforcing their society's foundation. Searching for something but not knowing what.

Man has always been searching for the key to keep society from having to go through the turmoil of collapse which forces him to have to rebuild his civilizations. The process of civilizations stepping back two steps in order to begin the process of stepping forward three is a traumatic one of souls. It has, however, been necessary. One that clears out the old to make way for the new.

The more advanced and populous the civilizations, the greater the collapse, and in turn the greater the energy needed to rebuild the civilization back to the level once obtained in order to allow for the growth beyond. The more populous the civilizations became, the more traumatic the collapse. Our society is so large, so interconnected globally, so tied together that a collapse will be a trauma of epic proportions. World War II with 50,000,000 killed will be nothing in comparison.

Take heart, the fall of civilization as we know it may be inevitable, but so is the fortitude of man. Sure it would be a traumatic event for the generations that have to face the collapse, but be assured the future generations are, as in the past, well-equipped with the inner conviction that there is hope for a better future, there is a purpose for man and men.

Even though Nostradamus predicts that although the collapse of civilization as we know it is in the future for us, he predicts at the same time, the rise of a magnificent civilization after ours that will bloom fabulously for thousands of years to come. History indicates that our present civilization will collapse. It has always been so. Now I have to grant you that although Nostradamus concurred, Nostradamus also added a qualifier, an interesting qualifier at that. The qualifier, ". . .unless we change." What does that mean, "change"? Haven't we changed, haven't we gained new knowledge? Absolutely. But we haven't changed a lot. We still cling to our shortsighted personal wants and desires. We have no concept of the big picture.

What big picture? The big picture of who man is, what his purpose is, and who we are as individuals. We have been searching for these answers since the beginning of our rational presence on this blue and white globe. We have searched the earth inside and out looking for it. We gazed in the heavens in awe and dreamed of going there to see if we could find the answer in its beauty and seemingly unbounded size.

All the while we have searched and wondered, we have toiled through life using hope to keep us going as men. Using faith to lift us above despair and pain. We have delighted in the optimism and promise our religions have provided us. Religions, institutions, devised by men to keep the concept of hope alive. The inner gut feeling that man has a purpose. That man was created by God. That man will once again see the other side of the boundaries of this reality. An inner gut feeling that says we will all be together once again.

But this concept of life after death is not one that just drives society. It is one that drives the very primitive desires of man himself. Scientists in their desire to maintain rationality, have put forward the concept that man, like all animals, reproduces offspring because of a primitive need to continue his gene pool. Nice theory, but it doesn't cut it. Man is a unique animal upon this biosphere. He is the only rational being of which we are aware. There is no doubt that the drive to reproduce is definitely a strong drive in man, but, as a rational animal it is also one filled with hope and optimism.

Each act of bringing a new individual into this world is proceeded by the belief that this world will be a better place for our children. The belief that our children will continue on with mans' purpose in this reality. The belief that we will someday join those that preceded us and be joined by those that are to come.

Nostradamus understood what it takes to keep a civilization from following in the path of all civilizations before it. He understood the fact that the foundation of human convictions built upon faith used to be enough of a foundation upon which to build civilizations. He also understood civilizations had, and always would, outgrow the foundation of faith unless something changed.

Does that mean we should abandon faith? Abandoning faith would be demolishing the very foundation upon which all civilizations were built. Demolishing faith would not be changing, that would be destroying and restarting. The demolishing, the collapsing of civilization, is what Nostradamus implied would happen to today's civilization if we did not change. No, the answer must lie elsewhere. The answer must lie where man has always been looking but never been able to find what he has been searching for. We must look to where man has historically been driving himself in order to put his soul to rest in terms of who he is, does he really have a purpose in life, and just what that purpose is.

Solving this universal question of man would cause a change in men of proportions never before seen. If man found he had a logical purpose, a task to perform, he would look at this reality in an entirely different light. Society would transform itself from one of having men build it to becoming a tool of men, to a tool needed to accomplish their tasks in this reality.

But wouldn't this concept undermine religions of the world? Only if it is self-serving and had an agenda of moving any one particular religion into the forefront over the others. This by definition alone would eliminate a philosophy as a universal philosophy. That in itself would be counterproductive to the very meaning of the words universal philosophy.

Knowing there is a purpose to life and what it might be, knowing that there is a purpose for all men, each and every one, would make men reevaluate society as a whole. Men would no longer expand, refine, and improve society as a random series of actions, but would take on the task of expanding, refining, and improving society because it was necessary to have society the best it could be in order to better accomplish the journey of present and future souls.

Men would have a common goal that would be universal for all of them. Men would become brothers through a common purpose. Doing what is right in life would become an act of reason, not just of faith. Man would have what it needs, a foundation for his foundation of faith.

Faith: would it disappear as one of man's primary sources of strength? Hardly; it would grow. For although reason and logic would lead men into an understanding of what their purpose in life might be, the key word would still remains, "might". As logical, as rational, as all encompassing as a universal philosophy might be, it would, at this point in our development, still be unprovable. It would still take faith to reinforce the logic.

Religions: would they disappear and evolve into something different? Quite the contrary; they would be strengthened in the recognition of the need for them as guides for men to follow in order for men to fulfill their purpose in life. A life that now would have more meaning than ever before. Religions would act as newly invigorated institutions of men, energized with the knowledge that they were "right" all this time. Reinforced with the knowledge that their struggle to remain true to the convictions of man, regarding where he came from and to where he is going, would be exhilarating beyond words.

A social paradox would be blown away. The paradox of why so many religions, so many faiths, so many religious traditions and doctrines exist. Instantaneously at the same time the understanding of why so many religions evolved, an understanding would materialize of why it is crucial to maintain those differences. Why religions must not coalesce as one through the process of conformity.

Religions would be thrown back from moving to conform, as they are doing now, to being proud they are different. Religions would cultivate their differences and stand tall within them. For the first time in mans' history, religions would be working together, would feel security in themselves and recognize the importance of their individuality. They would see that they are all the same already in that they provide a universal understanding of the connection of God and man. They would recognize that they are the same in that they all provide a set of directions for souls to follow, a common direction.

On the other hand, religions would also recognize that their individual uniqueness is crucial to provide the variety of homes necessary for the multitude of unique souls traveling through the journey of life. Souls need a place to rest and religions provide just that place. They are unique entities. There are too many unique souls in this reality to make it possible to create one religion that would feel like home to all of them at the same time. Unique souls need a unique place of refuge. There needs to be a place of peace for every uniquely colored soul. Religions need a universal philosophy in order to get along with all religions as badly as man himself needs a universal philosophy in order to get along with all men.

How is a universal concept "change"? Is this what Nostradamus was referring to when he spoke of change? To determine if this is the concept to which Nostradamus was referring would take more scholarly people than I to interpret. One thing is certain, philosophers, scientists, men in general have been seeking answers to their eternal significance for a long time.

It is also obvious that we have never had such a philosophy. There is no doubt that such a philosophy would change men and their behavior if it was truly accepted. It would only build, not destroy. It would only reinforce, not undermine. It would only benefit, not harm.

So why don't we have a universal philosophy? Because no one has been putting out a concrete effort to look. No teams representing all branches of faiths and knowledge have been assembled to look for a universal philosophy because one has never existed before.

It's time to get off our rocking chairs and begin working. It's time to stop sitting around lamenting over how civilizations have always collapsed and wondering when the same thing will happen to ours.

What a dilemma. Man builds social institutions to reinforce his convictions with such rigidity, they cannot bend. He embellishes each with masterful intricacies of uniqueness and then forgets to build bridges connecting them. Institutions of religion, science, mysticism, the arts, family, government, economics, research, recreation, on and on it goes. Man is truly a marvelous animal. He just forgot one thing: the bridges.

Each has so much to offer the other. Each working together could provide an insight into a universal philosophy that would knock the socks off mankind. A universal philosophy that would shiver at the sight of mans' wasting other mens' souls. Wasting their souls by paying them not to assist in the dream of men. Paying them to sit and do nothing – and if they want to do something, refusing to pay them anything.

A universal philosophy would shiver in the tidal wave of awareness of men being forced to abandon their families in the belief that their families would be better served by the cold inhuman form of government assistance. We have abandoned souls, demeaned souls, and used souls for our own self esteem, through our social creations. A dilemma? There is no doubt. We have created social institutions out of good intent with no understanding of how to make them work for man. Actions with good intent formulated in a vacuum of ignorance and ending up to be a scourge upon the very souls of men they were intended to help.

But this was no different than before; this is just how other civilizations operated. There was no change in our operation process since the foundation remained the same. Unfortunately, the foundations of the past had no foundation and eventually crumbled.

We have a choice: go on as man did in the past or change. The change has to be unique. The change has to involve the very foundation of man and what he has stood for over the course of his history.

The change has to be the basic of basics. The change has to be in how man looks at himself. The change has to be how man looks at fellow travelers. The paradox is that the change that must take place is a change into the mode of understanding so we can in fact maintain our existing underlying principles, principles that man has held dear through all these millennia. The change has to be a building of a new foundation under the one we have now. It must be a foundation that strengthens the one we have in place today. It would be a foundation that supports us for years to come.

This is not a new idea. The concept of a universal philosophy has been discussed by many philosophers in the past as well as today, Steven Hawkings being one of them. But what is different about today, why do we need a universal philosophy today when we never had one before? We need a universal philosophy because society is becoming so burdened down with new knowledge and new insights that faith is on the verge of buckling under the weight.

We must build a new foundation under our present foundation of faith. We must build a foundation – a universal foundation

– that connects man to God, a foundation that will carry man into Nostradamus' new world: a changed world.

"In Summary"

Hope Is What Carries Civilizations Forward

All Civilizations Have Eventually Collapsed

The Next Collapse Will Be Unimaginable

Man Is More Than An Animal

Nostradamus Told Us What To Look For

Religions Need A Universal Philosophy As Badly As Man

Change Is Not Easy

A Voluntary Change Is Less Traumatic Than A Change Caused By Collapse

"Under the spreading chestnut tree, The village smithy stands; The smith a mighty man is he with large and sinewy hands, And the muscles of his brawny arms Are strong as iron bands, He earns whatever he can, His brow is wet with honest sweat, And looks the whole world in the face, For he owes not any man."

Henry W. Longfellow

Chapter 19:
Class Status: Social/Occupational/Economic
♦
Illusions All, Perpetuated By The One's It Hurts The Most

Social, occupational, economic status are all created by man to suit his own needs and, oddly enough, meeting the needs of all involved whether positively or negatively. Status runs in a continuum from one extreme ("lowest") to the other ("highest"). Even the ones at the very lowest level have a stake in the continuation of the status illusion.

Those at the upper end of the continuum (status) perpetuate the illusion of the status in order to continue reaping its benefits. In addition, they perpetuate the continuation of the lower levels of the continuum in order to muster support for the continuation of their own level.

Those at the middle levels support the upper levels in order to continue to reap their benefits and to muster the support of both the upper and lower levels.

Those at the very lowest end have no allies and no choice but to live with the system until it breaks down. This they will relent to as long as the status system continues to benefit their journey through life also, as long as their quest for accomplishment of their souls is not denied.

The status systems do break down. Sometimes the system breaks down relatively quickly, sometimes it takes a longer time. Break down it always will, however, for it goes against the very concept of man, regarding both who he really is and what his purpose is in this reality in which we live.

Man is God Himself and his purpose is to create knowledge through experiences and creativity. This, then, he brings back to God, Himself, to expand God's omniscience, omnipotence, and omnipresence since God cannot, by definition, do so Himself as Himself. Thus, if all men are, in essence, God Himself, then all men are truly equal, just having different capabilities to use while in the machine they occupy. The status given them is a burden, not a pleasure, for the greater the status the greater the responsibilities and the greater the risk of obtaining a negative ripple effect in the realm beyond our reality.

The status level system, regardless of the mask it takes, economic, social, occupational, etc., is mans' attempt to duplicate the subconscious misconstrued perception he has of himself as an entity. The misconception that one man has more significance over another in the journey through reality.

The greatest of all leaders, thinkers, and creators from Einstein, Beethoven, Rembrant, Caesar, Nostradamus, etc., are well known. They are placed on pedestals by men as well they should be. The problem is that they are placed on pedestals for the wrong reasons, which leads to the creation of various forms of status systems in our society.

Great creators, thinkers, and doers are placed upon pedestals, because it is thought they independently overcame adversities, gained new insights, and created unique perceptions. How wrong. They in fact could never have attained their level of development without the aid of the men around them. People who produced their food. People who disposed of their wastes. People who built their shelters. And people who cared for their body's needs, surroundings, culture, and catered to their very souls.

"Great" people need to be placed on pedestals but not for the reasons we do. They need to be placed upon pedestals for two reasons.

First: they need to be placed high upon pedestals as symbols of what all men have attained. They need to be placed upon pedestals as reminders to all men, from the "lowest status" to the "highest" status, of just how far they have come as men in their quest for knowledge. They need to be placed upon pedestals to be seen so that men may literally use them as beacons in the night to give all men guidance in terms of what direction to pursue in their lives. They need to be placed upon pedestals in order to give religion and culture reinforcement in their attempt to provide man with the guidelines he needs to help him find the best way through the journey of his present reality.

Second: "great" creators, thinkers, and doers need to be placed upon pedestals as examples of what we would like to accomplish ourselves or what we would like our children to accomplish. Realistically, almost no one will reach these levels. But we can all take comfort in knowing we provided an environment for an Einstein to function, or sorrow in knowing we provided an environment for a Hitler to function, for we are equally responsible for both.

It is the "little" man that allows the "greater" man to gain his status and to accomplish his goals. There is no such thing as "little" or "greater" men. These are just status concepts. We all have important parts to play. Without each soul participating, steps we take, the quest to expand God's, our omniscience, omnipotence, and omnipresence, would never be accomplished.

Should we eliminate the various status systems? Some would say, "Yes" and others would say, "No". Some status systems facilitate, some hinder, mans' purpose in this reality. The ones that facilitate, we must keep intact but change our perception of them. As an example, we must view the wealthy status as a status that has its function but also has its responsibilities. This must be accepted by both those having been given this status and those having given the status (not only the levels above but just as importantly the levels below). We must realize that the status is there for a reason and has a function. We must realize that as long as that status is used for the good of the journey of all souls, it is serving its function. We must also realize that we cannot interfere with the soul occupying that position in its journey through life unless it is obviously interfering with the journey of other souls. We are not the ones to judge.

Different status levels and systems do become obsolete or abused, however. When this occurs, it is the duty of those that have given the level or system its authenticity to remove it. This does not mean just those occupying the "upper" levels but those occupying the "lower" levels as well have this obligation. It must not be done for personal gain but rather only for the good of all souls. This is not an easy task and should not be taken lightly by either group or by any individual, for we all have a purpose to accomplish in life and need to pursue that purpose not in a self serving fashion as perceived in society's perception. We need, rather, to pursue our purpose in a self serving fashion in the universal sense that we are all God, and we will all benefit from even one soul attaining the maximum attainment of its own personal purposes in life.

To this end we must all strive to attempt to attain our own purpose in life and to assist others to do the same. We must start to do this at the expense of selfishness and self serving actions. We must all strive to do this, accepting credit for and a deep sense of satisfaction in our roles concerning the mundane roles we play to the part we played in the accomplishments of the most visible souls such as Picasso, Bach, Galileo, and Luther.

They are all there, in the heavens. A great cheering section for all men, for all intelligence, for all souls. They are there rooting for the souls of the universe, the souls of all universes for they too will benefit from the success of all souls. They too are God as we are. They too will grow in omniscience, omnipotence, and omnipresence. By now they recognize, if they hadn't before, the vital role we all played in their roles.

They are all there: Scarlatte, Van Gogh, Plank, Edison, Buddha, Watts, Rutherford, Lewis, Dickens, Christ, Tolstoy, Confucius, Ghandi, Mandela, Dalai Lama, Moses. They are all rooting for the players on the field. Is this a game? Does this mean life is a game? By no means, for your soul will live with the results for eternity through the ripple effect. God Himself, you, yourself, will grow or not grow in omniscience, omnipotence, and omnipresence through your own efforts and the efforts of others. God, you, will be fully aware of the contributions you and all others made to the omniscience, omnipotence, and omnipresence. This will be your heaven. This will be your hell.

We must be careful not to destroy status systems that have taken the millennia to perfect to the degree they have been developed. We must not destroy them at the expense of others in order to advance our own selfish short purposes in this life. What a burden. What a responsibility. What purpose we all have to ourselves as well as to others. This is what is meant by: "It is easier for a camel to go through the eye of a needle, than for a rich man to enter into the kingdom of God."

And who are the "rich"? They are those at the higher end of the status continuum. Not the high end, the higher end. Higher is relative and simply means, "above". Any status is high compared to the one below it. Therefore, all levels but the 'lowest' one is "rich". Some more so than others.

We all are at the higher end of the status spectrum in one system or another. Status systems aren't just social, occupational, and economic. They exist in terms of man-made as well as natural. They run from the systems of economic to the physical. Status systems include: money, talent, intelligence, spiritual conviction, self esteem, social skills, family, love, joy, health, physical appearance, strength, physical perfection, religious and personal contentment, and moral convictions. The list goes on and on. Each of us has his own place in each of the systems. Each of us must work within these systems. Each of us must assist others with their weak points using our strong points.

None of us may judge others regarding the effectiveness of their efforts to use their strong points. None of us can be so presumptuous as to believe we are capable of understanding the myriad of interwoven experiences other souls have been exposed to which mold their personalities, needs, fears, ambitions, and desires. We have enough trouble understanding ourselves without understanding and judging others.

We can only assume when others are intruding upon the journey of other souls. We can only assume when others are advancing their own souls at the expense of others. We can only assume when others are threatening the advancement of all souls worldwide. Even then we have only our own perceptions by which to go. Even then we miss many blatant and horrific acts. Even then we make many mistakes through our own selfish wants and misguided pasts.

Judge we must from time to time, when other souls and our own are being directly affected. When only the soul of the individual is at stake, leave it alone: assist; encourage; act as a model, but leave it alone. The higher up you are on the status continuum, the more responsibility you have, the richer you are, and the harder it is for you "to pass into the kingdom of God", your kingdom. This is a figurative concept referring to the part of the afterlife men have wanted to be in and wanted to experience. Man has always recognized the concept that there is "a place" for all men.

Although you cannot literally shut yourself out of your own kingdom, you definitely can affect the afterlife your soul will experience. You definitely can affect how much good, "the kingdom of heaven" and how much bad, "the depths of hell" you will experience in the afterlife.

The higher up on the status continuum you are, the more people you can and will affect. This in turn means the more souls you will have to confront and experience in the afterlife. Your status should affect your actions for your actions will affect directly the number of deep, deep cold souls that pass through yours in the afterlife and in like terms the number of warm souls that will pass through your soul's consciousness through the ripple effect.

Use your status wisely. It will have grave significance for you into eternity itself. It will never leave you or your consciousness for they are both what is known as the soul. Just as significantly, your actions in relation to your status, will be common knowledge to all souls throughout all eternity, forever, and you will be fully aware of this in the eternity to come.

Do what's right with your status in this reality. You will have to fuse with many souls in eternity. You will have to look into the very eyes of an infinite number of souls for an infinite length of time. Souls you have directly and indirectly affected throughout life will place their mark upon you through the ripple effect. God help your soul. God help my soul. God help Himself.

Status

Social/Occupational/Economic Illusions

"In Summary"

Class Status Was Created By Man, Not God

Man Is God

God, We, Our Souls Have No Need Of Status

Society Has A Need For Status

Pedestals For Men Are There For The Wrong Reason

We Are Truly Equal In The Journey Of Life

You Have A Responsibility To Use Your Status Wisely

"My atheism, like that of Spinoza, is true piety towards the universe and denies only gods fashioned by men in their own image, to be servants of their human interests."

George Santayana
Soliloquies in England 1922

Chapter 20: Atheism

♦

The Atheist Has A Soul, He Too Is God But Yet A Lonely Place He Occupies

So you're an atheist. Nice. And that's the way it should be. Being a Buddhist, Hindu, Muslim, Christian, Jew, Taoist, etc., does not, nor will it ever, change what the universe is. It does not change what the creator is. What is, is. We cannot change that and being an atheist will not change that either. What will be, though, does not need to be. We do influence what is to come. Being an atheist will not destroy the world.

If your comfort zone for the soul lies in atheistic beliefs, so be it. You cannot change that. People should respect that. What has our world come to when a man cannot declare who he is without fear of rejection of himself and more importantly those near and dear to him.

God is God, life is life, nature is nature, the soul is the soul. None will change because you are an atheist. You have a purpose in life just as the rest of us do. You have a quest for your soul just as the rest of us do. The rest of us need to respect that and be grateful that you have the courage to stand up and express your convictions.

You are the faction in society that keeps the rest of us honest. You are the faction in society that forces the majority into introspective thought regarding what our convictions really are and mean. You are the faction in society that helps us see that other religions and convictions may have merit.

You have a purpose, a function in society and no one can take that away from you. You keep the churches, religions, governments, and cultures in a tolerance mode through your questioning of their beliefs, for if they cannot show compassion toward you, where does the line of noncompassion and lack of understanding become drawn?

Be cautious in your declarations, however, for you too are susceptible to the ripple effect just as the rest of us are. You too will have to face the souls you influence in this reality. You too will feel the souls of other's lives flow through your soul in an unending parade of realization of the actual impact of your soul's journey and the direct and indirect influence it had upon others. Tread with caution, for you affect many in your stark unorthodox stands. Be gentle, for your message is potent and easily shakes the foundations of other souls. Know your purpose and seek success carefully.

You have your beliefs, express them. You have your doubts, display them openly. You have your convictions, stand up for them. At the same time, however, you have no right to destroy the beliefs of others. You have no right to attempt to convert others to your thoughts and convictions at the expense of their thoughts and convictions, at the expense of the thoughts and convictions of their ancestors, at the expense of the thoughts and convictions of their culture.

Model, debate, question, demand respect for yourself, but do not diminish, belittle, begrudge, and disrespect the beliefs of others. Do not destroy the homes, the religions, of the souls of others. You are the faction that represents merely the middle of the religious continuum but you have been branded the unreligious, the evil faction, the far extreme. Religions have done this to you in fear of what you represent. They fear they cannot answer your questions. They fear they cannot withstand your logic.

Religions have little faith in themselves. Part of the reason is because there is a little atheism in all men, regardless of how fervently they deny this. Religions run in the form of a religious conviction continuum. Different individuals are on different points of this continuum. Men have been lead to deny the truth about their own atheistic doubts because they have been lead to believe that to admit it would commit them to eternal hell. How ludicrous for individuals to accept the idea that what they are mentally and what they feel mentally would lead them to be punished by eternal damnation.

Granted, how one expresses this doubt can have everlasting consequences. Accepting a religious conviction, declaring that same religious conviction, and then becoming a leader within that very same religious group, places a responsibility upon oneself that will stretch into infinity. Your actions at each point along the line of your journey become more and more influential and the repercussions to one's soul become more and more acute. To gain major status in the religious arena for example and then declare your conversion to atheism on a whim should not be taken lightly. The ripple effect can be quite immense.

Do not use people, status, power, notoriety or your own weaknesses to create shock waves for the sake of shock waves or to raise your level of public exposure. You may want to bask in the limelight of controversy in this reality, but don't forget you will have to bask in the realization of the true and total effects for eternity.

Society needs to reevaluate its understanding of atheism. Atheists have been portrayed as the far extreme. In fact, they represent the middle of the religious continuum. The far extreme is represented by the worshipers of evil, the satanists, the devil worshipers, the souls that have dedicated themselves to the destruction of man who is God Himself.

The far extreme drives itself toward confrontation of man's purpose in life. The far extreme embraces concepts that not only go contrary to man's purpose but attempts to destroy that very purpose. They go beyond the atheist in questioning and denying to actively attempting to actually destroy mans' success at attaining his quest in this reality. The lack of a purpose, the lack of a universal cohesive philosophy, leads them to reject their own sense of deja vu, intuition, cultural teachings in favor of an approach of deliberate denial in the hopes of being swiftly punished by a greater force they deliberately taunt. They look for this swift punishment by a greater force in the hopes of being shown wrong while in this present reality so that their fears of being right may be unequivocally proven wrong. This, they believe, will give them concrete proof to believe.

But believe what? Man has yet to develop that universal philosophy the Satanists, the atheist, the religious yearn to find. Man has yet to formulate the universal philosophy that will incorporate all aspects of men with respect and tolerance. Man has yet to coalesce the thinking of all men to date into a comprehensive understanding that will provide legitimacy to all true religions while still demanding each to retain its own personality.

Man has, to the contrary, moved in the opposite direction of attempting to provide legitimacy to all religions through conformity. A process which will in the end prove to be the undoing of religions themselves, which will destroy the homes of the souls, which will in turn lead to restlessness, intolerance, confusion, and disorientation of the souls of this very planet. The end result could be more devastating than any threat of nuclear, biological, or conventional war could ever be for this would lead to an expansion of psychological violence, a violence we have been seeing only in its infancy.

Atheism is not our problem. Men feel what they feel. Men are what they are. All men deserve respect and tolerance as long as they are not interfering with the journey of other souls. All men deserve respect because they are all machines of souls on journeys through this reality with the purpose of expanding knowledge and the very being of the omnipotent, omniscient, omnipresent force, themselves.

Our next opponent to face in this reality is psychological violence. Its growth is becoming rampant and it needs to be faced. We cannot face it naked and alone for it will engulf us and swallow each soul whole one at a time. We need a weapon in our arsenal to counter the geometric growth of psychological violence. That weapon is an understanding of mankind's purpose in the total scheme of things. That weapon is an understanding of both the fact that each man has a purpose and what that purpose actually is. This can only come if we garner and coalesce our knowledge; historic thoughts, insights, and training; commonalities of faiths; instincts; and deja vus; and then mold them from a universal philosophy, a new weapon to be used to unite all men, eliminate prejudice, and introduce tolerance as the mainstay of society.

A universal philosophy: the next development for man before he reaches for the stars. If we don't make it to the stars? Well, it will not be the end of our universe. It will not be the end of reality. There are other souls out in the heavens occupying other life forms that will continue the quest of expanding the omnipotent, omniscient, omnipresent force. We just won't be a part of it. How sad for us.

There is much to do. There is much to accomplish. We will need the contributions that all souls can make. We will need to act as a team. We will need to discard jealousy, hate, greed, selfishness, vengeance, violence, etc., and embrace tolerance, universal goals, respect, brotherly caring for each and every soul, for each and every machine the soul occupies, and for each and every home (religion) of the soul.

And where does the atheist stand in all this? Right in the middle of the religious continuum. A very difficult place to be indeed.

Atheism / Religion

The Atheist Also Has A Soul

"In Summary"

For Some Men, The Soul's Comfort Zone Is Atheism

Atheists Have A Journey To Travel Also

Heaven And Hell Are Not Entered Through What One Feels

Heaven And Hell Are A Product Of Action

Atheism Is A Precarious Position

Psychological Violence, Our New Worry

Being In The Middle Is A Difficult Place To Be

> *"In carrying on your government, why should you use killing (the unprincipled for the good of the unprincipled) at all? Let your evinced desires be for what is good, and the people will be good. The relation between superiors and inferiors is like that between the wind and the grass. The grass must bend when the wind blows across it."*
>
> Confucius (551 – 479 B.C.)
> *The Confucian Analects,* 12:1

Chapter 21: War/Abortion

♦

Take Care Of Your Own Soul

Men so like to poke into the business of other people. If it isn't in terms of telling them how to live, what to do, how to act, what's normal, what's proper, what's moral, or what religion is the true religion, then it's when to kill and when not to kill. The philosophy introduced in Part I of this book provides some insight as to what is and isn't acceptable in the case of both war and abortion.

Why place both together in one section? Because they are both analogous in nature. Both involve killing individuals. Both, in recent times, have involved billions of people. Both have created tremendous turmoil within contemporary society. Both have moral and religious connotations applied to them in much the same conflicting manner. And lastly, both have had no resolution brought to bear in terms of a long-term, nonconflicting consensus of the population.

What's the problem that we are unable, as rational individuals, to resolve these issues? It would seem that most of the problem in trying to come to terms with them lies in the fact that we have no rudimentary concept of our purpose in life as individuals or as a species. In short, we do not have a complete universal philosophy regarding the meaning of life and where we fit into the picture of life's meaning. We, therefore, have nothing to act as a monolithic anchor to which we can consistently orient our actions in terms of individual, local, or global reevaluation of our past historical behavior.

If one accepts the basics of "the philosophy":

1. God is God
2. Our souls and the souls of each and every individual are a piece of God
3. God created the universe as a creative lab
4. Our purpose is to expand God's knowledge base
5. We will have to live with the repercussions of our actions (Ripple Effect)

then an obvious and simple solution becomes apparent. The solution is two-fold in nature.

1. We have no right to kill under any circumstances, and 2. we have no right to interfere with the right of the individual to fulfill their purpose in the scheme of reality. We must jealously guard these rights of the individual even if it means, as a last choice, we must take the life of another. This does not mean we have the "right" to take a life; we just may have no other option.

Ah, the simplicity but the complexity, the obvious conclusion but the erroneous logic, the deftness at which we grasp at the obvious but the disheartenment we shall feel as we withdraw in disgust.

WAR

We should start with war since it has been with man since man has been a unique species. War is the process of killing in order to accomplish a goal: territorial expansion, economic gain, imposing one's moralistic values, expanding one's power status, maintaining one's pride, or just foolish lack of communication. All erroneous reasons. Killing is killing and destroys the temple of a soul. Each cuts short the development of a soul in its quest of accomplishing its purpose in life.

Does this mean we must never protect ourselves or our fellow men in a confrontation that could lead to our own death or even the death of another? If the party initiating the problem is attempting to interfere with the rights of another to pursue their own purpose in life, then we have the right to interfere. In fact one could say we have an obligation to interfere. Does this mean we should become involved in every violent conflict between nations worldwide? No. We may try to influence other nations in peaceful, ideological, economic, and cultural manners, but not through violent means.

One may then ask how we can, in all good conscience, allow thousands of our brothers to die in conflicts of violence. We cannot fight every fight on earth, nor can we resolve all men's ideological, cultural, or religious disagreement. We can, however, attempt to persuade them to live together in peace, be tolerant of one another, and respect each individual's right to make decisions. We can, through example, show them the technological, social, and economic advantages of working as equals. We can show them how to develop a society that maintains the rights of all and supports the concept of respect for each and every person.

How do we do this? We develop a complete, universal, understanding of each man's purpose in life and man's role in the scheme of things. Once established, the universal philosophy becomes a guide post for laws, social actions, and individual actions toward others.

Can this universal philosophy be based upon a particular religion? No, it must be based upon the universal commonality of all religions that are truly religions, laws of nature that touch the souls of all men.

Under this premise, would we have had the right to intervene in the world conflict in World War II? Yes, since it involved protecting and upholding our beliefs in the rights of the individual. Who would make these monumental decisions? Our leaders with the support of our citizens. The decisions should not be drawn into lightly, for those very decisions will affect the souls of men and we will live with the results of our decisions for eternity through the ripple effect.

Each man will live for eternity with the results of his action in war, action that leads to killing other men and thus terminating the quests of their souls. This leads us to the question, does any man have the right to encourage, force, or enlist another to participate in war without the full consent of the man who is to aid in or directly participate in the killing of other men?

The answer is no. To do so jeopardizes the soul of the man encouraging the killings. That is not, however, the reason enlisting others to kill is unacceptable, for each man is responsible for his own soul. What is unacceptable is enlisting other men to kill at the risk of leading them to jeopardize their souls through your influence. Thus, in war, each soul needs to be allowed to rationalize its own reason for participating or not participating in a war since each soul will live with the results of its decisions for eternity.

If wars are just, men will rise up and voluntarily participate in great enough numbers to defeat the negative forces attempting to spread their dominance.

ABORTION

A war? Yes. It involves a global conflict, hundreds of nations, billions of people, and hundreds of millions of temples for the soul, religious fanaticism, and personal inner turmoil and conflict within billions of individuals.

Expending the energy to fight such a battle becomes inefficient in terms of accomplishing the purpose of the species as well as doing nothing but raising further perplexing paradoxes. If we prevent people from making their own decisions regarding the issue of abortion and if we do not respect their right to make these and other decisions, then where do we stop at making the decisions for them? And just who do we think we are if we think we have the right to force people to do things in life that will affect them for eternity?

Do we then start to prohibit birth control on the premise it eliminates the potential of other temples for souls? Do we discourage small families since they limit the overall number of people on earth and thus could potentially limit the growth of souls attempting to fulfill their function in the cosmos? Do we limit families since this in turn could lead to a higher quality of life which in turn could lead to a growth of knowledge and exploration of the universe? Do we limit who can have children since some potential parents may not have what someone perceives to be the right parental characteristics? The list goes on forever. The only solution: have faith in the individual and respect their integrity to do what is right for themselves, knowing they will be the ones to live with the results into eternity.

We must respect their decision, even if it goes against our own values, as long as it does not interfere with the rights of others. We have no idea of the personal turmoil, problems, or needs of the soul at work in the body of another person. We have no right to judge their decisions. We will never know of what importance the terminated soul may have had to the world. The soul may have accomplished its purpose just through the short existence it had experienced. After all, a life involving 8 minutes of conception is relatively as long as that of an 8 month old fetus; which in turn is relatively as long as that of a 1 year old child; which in turn is relatively as long as that of a one hundred year old man.

If all lives are relatively of equal length, then why not just encourage suicide or the termination of all people terminally ill, handicapped, "dumb", ugly, unemployed, white, or bald? Because they are all homes for souls. They all contain souls with a purpose and we have no right to encourage the annihilation of any soul's journey in life.

We must encourage the alternative to termination of the temple of the soul. We have no right to shorten the time needed for the soul to accomplish its task. We have an obligation to support, encourage, and reach out a hand filled with hope, love, and brotherhood to all souls regardless of social stigmas and labels pinned on them by society.

Interfere with abortion? No. Supply alternatives? Yes. Discourage abortions through the imposition of guilt? No. Everyone must make their own difficult decisions in life. We must respect these decisions even if they do not reflect our values and as long as they do not disrupt the rights of others.

But abortions affect the rights of others, anti-abortionists would say, but the actual answer to this response is maybe and maybe not. We are not in a position to fight this war and come to a universal, all-encompassing conclusion regarding this issue. Nor are we able to judge which situations should or should not be included under the umbrella of our moralistic judgment. No one but the mother has the right to make this decision.

The father may have helped in the conception, but the mother must bear the brunt of the burden of the decision into eternity. Bringing the fetus into the world may or may not be advantageous to the world or to the fetus, but only the mother will fully bear the brunt of knowing for eternity the results of her decision.

Even the parents of the mother have no right to make the decision for her. Parents of a minor child have every right, however, to be informed, for they have an obligation to nurture, guide, and assist the child they have brought into this world or for whom they have accepted the obligation of raising. Even so, they may not make the final decision for the mother, nor impose their decision upon her through guilt. They may reassure, encourage, and commit themselves to assistance, but the final decision must come from the mother and following that, everyone in society, including the father of the child and parents of the mother, must provide support for her decision and to her.

We do not have enough information regarding the individual fetuses, future lives of the fetus, personal needs and turmoils of the mother, and understanding of our purpose in life or the universe to fully comprehend the problem regarding abortions, let alone answer the myriad of questions surrounding it. Thus to impose our individual decisions and morality upon other individuals involved is not only judgmental but egotistical. All we can do is say, "I'm not absolutely sure what's right", and then extend an earnest hand of comfort, respect, and support for whatever decision a mother finally makes.

This conflict based upon personal belief of when a soul enters the body is one that cannot be resolved at this point in time with certainty. We have no idea of when a soul enters the body, the machine of man. We do not know if it is at conception, 1 day later, 1 week, 1 month, 3 months, 6 months, or even before conception as the egg drops from the ovary. All we can do is go by what we sense. Maybe it would be at the time of the production of brain wave patterns in the fetus.

We will have to come to some census in order to resolve the conflict. Experts more knowledgable than I will have to work this problem out. I am not trying to shirk the issue here. I just don't know the answer. Whatever the decision becomes, however, society, souls each and every one, better be ready to put their money, compassion, and energy where their conviction lies.

People in society, souls, should never be forced to pay for something they morally disagree to. Governments extracting money from people to fund actions the people abhor is immoral. It is no different than one soul committing violence against another. It is just as insensitive; it also is an action contrary to a universal philosophy. It too is a self-serving action detrimental to the souls that governments supposedly are to protect.

Again I must reiterate, we must have faith in the individual and respect their integrity to do what is right for themselves, knowing they will be the ones to live with the results into eternity. Who would better know than the mother of her own child. Respect, tolerance, trust, and faith in our fellow souls are the key words regardless of the decisions made by the mother herself and may wisdom be their guide for they shall live with the results for eternity.

War / Abortion

Take Care Of Your Own Soul

"In Summary"

We Have No Right To Tell Others When And When Not To Kill

No One Has The Right To Kill Another

War Is Killing

We Must Protect The Rights Of All Souls Even If It Means Death

We Cannot Resolve All Wars Of Life

We Don't Know When The Soul Enters The Body

Society, Souls, Better Be Ready To Put Their Money, Compassion, And Energy Where Their Convictions Lie

We Need Faith And Trust In Our Brothers

"Often my creative life has seemed like a long tunnel, dark and damp. And sometimes I wondered whether I could live through it . . . But I did."

Ai Qing (b. 1910)
Chinese poet,
who suffered under Maoist rule

Chapter 22: Suicide

♦

So You Don't Feel So Good?

Feeling pain, pain so deep the thought of eternal blackness is a comfort. Emotional pain. Pain so deep and silent you would like to feel the security of the peaceful blanket of eternal night that would shut out the pain of day.

Seeing your life reaching its peak and all your reasons for living seem to be over and gone? Yearning for a purpose but unable to envision any other than the opportunity to take a long appealing rest? Missing that special someone who is now gone? Wrenched from your being like an arm cruelly jerked off your body, leaving bloody torn fragments in its place. The emotional pain and loss is indescribable but knowing it, you would be more than willing to take the physical pain of the lost arm over what you now feel.

Feeling you have reached the end of your time. Life has been good but now, after decades and decades of putting energy into it, everyone seems to have left and so little time remains that it seems impossible to have any significance, so why bother?

My heart goes out to you. I know how you feel. I haven't been to all these places, but I've been to some. I understand. I sympathize. I empathize. Just writing about it makes my heart sad, my eyes moist, and my soul heavy. I wish I could give you relief and say, "go gently into that good night", but I cannot. I wish I could say "go in peace" to your desired destination, but I cannot. I wish I could tell you, "you have put up the good fight and you have earned your rest", but I cannot.

God help me, for what I am about to tell you will apply to me also. If it helps you to understand that I have been there, all the better. I want you to understand that I in no way would ever prejudge a suicide attempt; I would only feel a heavy heart from it. People have no right to make judgments about people who commit suicide, for they have no idea of the physical, or worse, mental pain, other people are experiencing. But this does not give you the clearance to take the step of terminating your own life.

If there is truly an afterlife, and if we truly are a significant portion of it, and if our significance comes from our learning experiences here on earth, then we need to do all we can to extend our natural lives, as much as we can, in order to accomplish our purpose in life. Does this mean extending our life beyond what is natural? No. What is natural with today's medical science or another individual? That is another topic of discussion.

What we do know, however, is what is not natural, in the sense that it would not occur without our direct intervention, and that is suicide.

I know you hurt and I know you feel really down, but you need to see that this is not the time to end your present life form. To do so would shorten your life on a negative point and prevent you from completing your life's purpose, which is to bring back to the Omniscience more knowledge. It would in essence mean that, in the long run, your next life consciousness would be less knowledgeable. I know this does not mean anything to you the way you feel right now, but remember, it will later.

In the next life consciousness, you will be aware of the shortcomings for which you were responsible. You will be fully aware of the lives you did not touch and the lives they in turn touched differently due to your absence, and how they in turn touched other lives differently, etc. Your affect upon other people is important and significant regardless of how small it might seem to you. Your taking your life will have an impact both upon yourself and many others directly and through the ripple effect. You will feel the ripple effect for all eternity of your loss to someone, your encouragement of others to not fight their battles, the cynicism you helped to perpetuate through your suicide in not just one man, but others they in turn touch as well in a myriad of other ways.

I'm truly sorry to lay this burden on you, but you must know. Life is short although it can seem an eternity, but live it we must. Oh, there are times we must let go, I do not mean to say otherwise. Part of living is knowing when to let go and to go in peace and go even with desire and anticipation. But this is different than your making the decision. This is accepting your having accomplished your end and being at peace with this. It is finding comfort in knowing there is something after death.

If it is nothing we go to, that in itself is something, meaningless perhaps, but something. This would indeed provide you with your peaceful blanket of darkness. It would also mean your actions would not be of any consequence, which in turn would only accentuate how ludicrous your action of suicide would be anyway. For to terminate your only existence has no meaning since your own existence is but short lived compared to the life of the universe.

Beware, however, if there is a life after death. For you will then experience it. You will then be living it literally and to go into it not only aware of, but literally experience, all your life's actions and their every ramification, regardless of how small, through the ripple effect.

You need to be made aware that to finish out your relatively short life is, in essence, no longer than to end it now. To live out your relatively short lifetime is, in essence, no longer than the length of time you have left to live. For one hour compared to one year, ten years, or even fifty years is much less than fifty years is to the five billion years the universe has been in existence. The significance of living out your life, as compared to taking it now, is one that will touch upon your comfort level in eternity itself and that is significant.

Take heart, for there is a positive side to this also, and that is, that time does truly seem to mend the heart and soul, whether through the time of living or whether through reaching our eternal rest. If you are in pain, physical or emotional, do not wait for life to unleash its forces on you. Seek out others around you and also others like yourself. Share with each other and comfort each other. You have much to give them and much to give mankind in your own significant manner. Remember, significance is a relative term. They in turn have much to give you. You both have much to learn. As impossible as it may seem, your purpose in life is not yet over.

I know your pain and my heart weeps for you as I say, "Go in peace."

You & I Together

Suicide

So You Don't Feel So Good?

"In Summary"

Pain In The Heart

Pain In The Mind

Pain To The Very Depths Of The Soul Itself

Bear It You Must

But Take Heart – Life Is Short

Will The Pain Subside?
For Some Yes, For Others No

But You Do Not Have The Right To Stop It

Your Soul Still Has A Purpose

> *"The life of man is long, perhaps longer than necessary. Or perhaps it is shorter than necessary?"*
>
> Nazim Hikmet
> 1902 – 1963
> Turkish Poet

Chapter 23:
Capital Punishment / Life Incarceration
♦
A Debt To Society Is A Debt Owed To Other Souls
It Can Never Be Repaid

Paying your debt to man or society. There is no way to begin to complete this payment since each crime involves not one debt but three: 1. the debt to the soul against whom the crime was committed, 2. the collective debt against mankind's loss, and 3. the debt against one's own soul. Lets discuss all three in terms of "the philosophy" and see where it leads us.

Society has ignored two of these debts, the emotional and mental damage to the victim as well as the loss to society. Society has ignored them partly because it cannot adequately measure them. This doesn't mean society is right to ignore these areas damaged and pretend it never happened, however. Acknowledging to the victim that society is aware of the damage inflicted upon them, as a minimum, provides the first step in comforting that very soul and alerts society and the one committing the act that there was more damage done than just the act itself.

Complete restitution is impossible to accomplish. Since one can never totally repair the damage one causes to another soul nor to the souls of society as a whole, why would society or men attempt to even extract this magnitude of a debt from another soul. Capital punishment is society's means of extracting what it considers to be the ultimate form of restitution. In actuality, it is no form of restitution at all. With this in mind, why would men seek out the termination of another man, knowing that all men, even the ones committing the acts against other souls, are actually pieces of God Himself, just as are all men?

Knowing this places an entirely different slant upon the concept of punishment. In a sense, the punishment one doles out becomes a punishment against oneself for we are truly all brothers as all religions teach. We are all pieces of the same God, we are all God Himself. This concept leads us to understand that the brotherhood of man is not a figurative statement but a literal one. In fact the term "man" must be replaced with "souls" for soon we will find other brothers in the heavens above us.

This then leads us away from random, vindictive punishment. It leads us away from attempting to extract a debt that cannot be repaid. It leads us to planned, purposeful actions against the transgressor. The actions we take against souls that damage other souls then becomes not punishment but rather an attempt to protect other souls. It is the attempt on the part of one soul to protect the journey of the souls of others and provide them the environment necessary for them to efficiently follow and attempt to succeed at accomplishing their purpose in life without interference.

This then leads to the need of finding ways to have the transgressor repair the damage to other souls. It leads to reevaluating what we perceive is and what isn't a crime against the journey of other souls. It helps us understand when we have a right to step into the journey of another and modify it and when we don't.

Accepting "the philosophy" as a foundation for religions, magnifies and clarifies the position of religious beliefs that all men are important, even the ones that commit acts against the journeys of other souls. Their journey through life is not to be taken lightly, nor is it to be allowed to interfere with the journeys of others.

The approach suddenly eliminates the concept of punishment and replaces it instead with concepts of restitution, protecting other souls from damage, placing an uncaring soul into an environment in which it can function but cannot damage other souls, forgiveness of unintentional or emotional acts, and requiring restitution but not at the expense of a soul's journey through life or its purpose in life.

So where does this lead us? One thing is for sure, it leads us dramatically away from capital punishment. As much as we would like to extract a pound of flesh, no one has the right to terminate the journey of another soul, relocate it, yes; alter its journey so that it is unable to damage other souls' journeys, yes; but terminate it, no.

"The philosophy" leads us to an entirely different outlook regarding the concept of punishment. It forces us to recognize we, each and every one of us, have a responsibility (that has very profound implications indeed when looking towards the ripple effect) to protect our brothers, other souls, in their journey through life. Judges, lawyers, policemen, social workers, jurors, jailers, and the list goes on; do not take your responsibilities lightly for you will feel the effect throughout eternity. "Feel?", yes feel and experience the results of your responsibilities through the ripple effect, not in a sense of punishment, just as a matter of fact.

Don't let others influence you to make decisions or take actions that you feel go against your convictions, for you and you alone will feel the effects of your actions through the ripple effect. You, and you alone will be held accountable for your decisions. There will be no excuses for your participation in a death sentence against another soul. The plea of not knowing what one's convictions are or that society had set the rules and you weren't responsible, will have no merit, for you participated and that's that, pure and simple.

On the other hand, releasing an individual that has committed an act against another soul, releasing a soul that will continue to damage other souls, will also be your responsibility. You alone will empathize fully, in every sense of the word with how your actions affected not only the one being judged, but how your actions affected the victim. It is a frightening thing to think that you will feel the results of the instigator's actions and victim's pain and future state of mind.

This may be a good time for you to reread the **ripple effect** in this book, not only to cause you to pause and reflect before acting upon things, but to give you encouragement and hope as well. Considering "the philosophy", just what kind of punishment or action may man, society, take against other souls? Ones of kindness, ones of tough love, ones of protection of society's other souls, ones that help other souls find hope and rebuild their faith in the souls of other men.

Killing a man will not do this. It provides vengeance but actually only damages other innocent souls involved in the termination process, ironically even the victim. Life incarceration, on the other hand, does not terminate any soul. It does not eliminate the ability of a soul to function and attempt to rectify the damage it has created. The perpetrators can still create, write, expand their minds, influence others directly in contact with themselves as well as those who may be potentially in contact with them. The perpetrators have much they can do, if they so chose, to start making amends for their actions.

Life incarceration by society has its disadvantages to both society and the perpetrator and should be used sparingly and only in the most extreme cases of concern for the welfare of other souls in society. It is expensive for one thing, and that weighs unfairly upon the innocent souls of society. For another, it places extreme limits upon the continuation of a soul's quest for fulfillment of its purpose in life, your purpose, my purpose, although it could well be argued that this may be the purpose of that particular soul's journey.

Life incarceration has its positive side, however. It protects other souls in this reality against souls that have no sense of value of the worth of an individual, the value of a soul, the importance of a soul's journey, purpose, in this reality. Life incarceration also allows the victim to find peace in knowing the perpetrator of heinous crimes will not be allowed to repeat their acts against others. Often these victims, the families and souls that had been in contact with the victim's soul, find certain acts to be so deplorable, so damaging, that knowing their own agony, they seek capital punishment since they know of no other manner to be certain that the violent acts will not be committed against others.

If society could assure them of true life incarceration, often they would find the same peace of mind that would allow them to put the matter behind them and move on with their grieving process and with life. It would allow them to move on in life without feeling that they will be responsible through their inaction for the damage of other souls. They will be able to let go of the guilt associated with not having followed through on the partial vindication for the loved one's hurt.

Society has been at fault regarding life incarceration as a means of protecting society. Society has been fickle. Life incarceration is not life incarceration in our society and twenty years of isolation from society is not twenty years. Society has sold its principles for the convenience of convenience. Plea bargaining, time off for good behavior, parole, etc., all are means of closing one's eyes to one's own convictions. All are means of compromising, trading, one's principles for convenience. A rather poor bargain considering the ripple effect.

New and expanded means of protecting society and other souls within society need to be developed and implemented. Electronic tethering for less acute crimes against the souls of others becomes a means of providing more latitude for the perpetrator to make restitution to the souls it damaged and to be less of a burden upon society. Restitution becomes a means in itself to rectify offenses against other souls and society.

All this calls for the reevaluation regarding how to handle the perpetrator. All this calls for the elimination of concepts such as short prison terms due to lack of facilities and leniency. Destruction of records after a perpetrator reaches eighteen, first time offense excuses, product of society defense, all would need to be reexamined in light of a universal philosophy. Absolution by society and the reevaluation of what are crimes and what are not crimes becomes a must.

Society too will have to reevaluate its responsibilities. It will no longer be able to use the excuse of money as a reason to terminate the home of a brother, terminate the journey of another soul in this reality. Society will have to use its resources to protect its fellow souls. Segments of society, such as the police officers, judges, and jurors living in isolated and protected sections of society, those protected from chronic violators of other men's journeys, will not be able ever again to ignore the less fortunate that have to live day in and day out with the chronic violators of other mens' souls. The manpower, the finances, and the facilities will have to be addressed in order to ensure the safety and protection of all our brother souls in this reality.

The manpower is there if we use it efficiently and stop accepting the concept that some people are not needed in society. We need to recognize that all people, all souls, are significant and of importance. That all souls have something to contribute to mans' purpose and their own purpose in this reality. We have to stop throwing money at portions of society in an attempt to encourage them to stay out of the way and vegetate (examples: welfare, unemployment, and incarceration). The money is there, for money is but a tool to help us disperse time, and time is there, if we view time as a gross commodity of all men placed in a common pool.

It's time we recognize the importance of all men. It's time we open the opportunity for all souls to participate in the journey of man through history. It's time we utilize the energy of all men in our quest to fulfill our purpose in this existence in reality. We are not here just to be here. We are here for a reason. We need to accept that reason and then begin to utilize all men efficiently in our attempt to accomplish that purpose. That means all men, even the ones that are chronic, obscene, and intentionally obstructionistic to the journey of other men's souls. The accomplishment of the purpose of men, the accomplishment of the purpose of an individual soul, is a difficult one, a neverending one. It is a quest that one man alone cannot accomplish. It is a quest that no man alone is supposed to accomplish. It belongs to all men, for all men are one.

Alone, we face the results of our responsibilities in the afterlife. Alone, we must make our decisions in life. Alone, we will see the results of our each and every action.

But together, as a species, we must forge through the journey of this lifetime, for it is in this lifetime, this reality, that our purpose lies. The purpose of God lies in this reality, not in his own existence. Men, each being a piece of God, therefore will find that their purpose in our present reality as well as our next reality lies in what we accomplish within this reality. Knowing this, how can we ignore the needs of the protection of our fellow men, our fellow souls? How can we allow many of our fellow souls to linger in a vegetative state while we go about the quest of our own soul?

There is so much to do, we need all men to assist. The journey to the stars, the journey to expand God's very omniscience, omnipotence, and omnipresence, the journey to expand our, mans', very omniscience, omnipotence, and omnipresence since we are in fact God Himself, is a neverending one. It benefits all men to provide the opportunity for all men to assist in the most efficient manner they can.

Capital punishment? Hardly; it goes against the very purpose of man and men. Life incarceration? Absolutely; but on a limited basis to protect the journey of souls. Electronic tethering and restitution? Definitely; to rectify the damage done to the journey of other souls and to reestablish the faith we have in the souls of men.

Be careful if you are responsible or even partially responsible for letting a violent soul loose into society, for it will come back to haunt you. You will feel the effects of your actions. You will live, in all sense of the words, the effects of your actions.

This is too much for any of us. We need a guide. We need past historical guidelines to relieve some of the pressure of finding the correct path to follow. We need religions to act as our guides, to provide the paths which we can follow as we move, together, through the journey of this reality.

Death Penalty / Life Incarceration

A "Debt To Society" Is A Debt Owed To Other Souls

"In Summary"

Vindictive Punishment Is At Odds With "the philosophy"

No One Has The Right To Terminate The Journey Of A Soul

Judgment/The Ripple Effect – Hand In Hand

Journeys Of All Souls Need To Be Protected

Life Incarceration Does Not Terminate A Journey

Money Is Not The Point

Reevaluation And Restitution

The Victims Need Closure

"Forgiving the unrepentant is like drawing pictures on water."

Japanese proverb

Chapter 24:
Letting Go/Forgiving
◆
An Injured Soul Must Be Set Free

A severance from something or someone that has made close contact with your soul is never easy. It takes time, time to let the reality of the loss sink in, time to grieve, time to be angry, and time to accept the loss. All of this is as it should be. We may be a piece of God infused into a human machine, but that is as it implies: we are, in this reality, human. As humans, we will experience human emotions, some of which may prove to be very intense in nature.

Death, murder, accident, rape, abuse, intimidation, are just some examples of traumatizing situations encountered by souls on their journey through life. Victims are not the only ones that are traumatized. The list of victims of each incident stretches over a broad spectrum. It involves family members, friends, spouses, children, future connections with souls, and souls not touched due to the negative influence imposed upon the victim.

It is in some of these situations that it is often very difficult, if not humanly impossible, to let go. It is in these cases where there may never be enough time available to allow the pain, anger, or guilt to subside in order to actually let go and move on with one's journey. Part of the difficulty is brought about by society itself. Society often ignores the victims of crimes and other forms of violent interactions of one soul to another. The victim is brushed aside in what society calls "looking out for the rights of the accused". Society, men, must look out for the accused. The accused may be innocent. We all want protection available to us if the occasion ever arises that we are the accused.

In today's society, the victim is often ignored in favor of the perpetrator. We brush the victim aside like an inanimate object. This then compounds the problems for the victim. We can do as much damage to the victimized soul as the soul that started the process in the first place. Often this is done out of insensitivity, inconvenience, lack of passion, or just because it is easier to ignore a compassionate soul than an antisocial aggressive soul.

Souls that are in the position of imparting damage to victims, such as police officers, judges, juries, prison personnel, doctors, nurses, spouses, neighbors should take their positions seriously. They no doubt have to deal with unscrupulous souls much of their day but they should never forget that they need to wear two hats.

It is understandably difficult to constantly be exchanging hats during the course of one's work, but it is crucial in these occupations and positions to be doing so. The tendency through enough exposure to the side of our society that has no concern for others is to take on that very trait. But that means that the victims become victimized twice. A twice ravaged soul is a soul that will carry a heavy burden into the next stage of reality. This burden will be poured out of the victim's soul soon after stepping over the threshold of this reality and into the next. It will be poured out of the victim's soul into the initiator's soul.

All the pain, hurt, anger, and recurring memories of the event will flow out of the victim and right into the very soul of the offender. From then on it will be the soul of the perpetrator that will carry the burden. It will be the soul of the perpetrator that will feel all the emotion generated by their own actions. The worst part is that it will not be felt for a finite amount of time, as was the case of the victim, but rather will be felt for all of eternity. This is the ripple effect.

This is not God's punishment, this is not the victim's punishment, it is just the result of the souls, all souls, once again blending in with God. For to become a part of God again will mean just what it states. It means becoming fully aware of what actions we took in this reality. Not only aware of it in terms of the fact that we did certain things, but also in terms of the actual emotions it generated within the victim as well as the people affected by the victim, etc., etc.

A universal philosophy such as "the philosophy" can help victims in two ways. First, it can help by making people who have to wear two hats realize why it is important for them to do so. It makes them understand that not to do so only causes the victim to become a double victim. The significance here is that the second hit taken by the victim was generated by people who thought themselves to be good-intentioned people.

The second manner a universal philosophy can help the victim is through providing the victim with a sense of peace. An understanding that they will not have to carry the burden of the emotion and flashbacks for all of eternity. The burden will shift. The burden will end up where it belongs and the victim can take some peace in the knowledge that it will not be a case of the victim punishing the perpetrator, rather it will occur just as a matter of fact.

Part of the problem that victims have resolving the conflict they feel within their souls in terms of "the incident", deals with guilt. Some of this guilt deals with the conscious and sometimes subconscious fear of victims that other souls in society could be damaged by the perpetrator in their journeys just as the victim was. Here, society is to blame. This means you are to blame, for you, society, allows the perpetrator endless access to resources, rights, and protections, all set up for them by you. You say, "I don't have any control of what goes on. I didn't want it that way. There is nothing I can do about it."

Sorry, you lose. Once one begins to realize that one is responsible for all of one's actions or lack of action, one begins to realize the significance of the ripple effect and the fact that support through time or money of specific organizations, agencies (governmental), individuals, etc. makes one partially responsible for the ripple effect of their actions. In other words, individuals in society are responsible for the society in which they live and will obtain the benefit or displeasure of receiving part of the burden of souls affected by that very society they support.

The bottom line is that victims will unload their soul's burden while on their way to becoming infused back into God and all the rest of us in society will obtain a piece of that burden due to our allowing society to let perpetrators be treated better than the victims. We will obtain a share of the guilt and turmoil victims feel because we allow the perpetrators to duplicate their crimes over and over again. This is part of the problem victims have. They know this occurs and find it frustrating and usually futile, despite their efforts to change this problem. This inability of traumatized victims to protect other souls from experiencing what they had to go through causes them to experience even more trauma. This is our fault. We are the ones that allow the process of victimization to continue. We, you and I, therefore, are going to have to shoulder the repercussions of that burden through the ripple effect.

"The philosophy" places a tremendous responsibility upon people (souls) in society. It also provides for massive incentives to follow the guidelines of mans' religions. Not necessarily one religion over the other, but rather recognizes the basic message of all. In other words, it acts as a foundation for our guides in life, for religions. Making people, souls, aware of their responsibilities and the repercussions of meeting them or not meeting them is not a negative thing. It is just what we need as we approach our next stage as a species reaching for our next journey, the stars.

"The philosophy" forces us to reevaluate our social stands, laws, restrictions, programs, concepts, and society's interactions with respect to the individual. "The philosophy" forces us to reevaluate the very purpose of society altogether. It refocuses the purpose of society from taking care of the individual to working to assist souls' journey successfully through this reality, to fulfill their purpose in life. This does not imply that society must give to a soul everything it wants. This would be no different than a parent giving a child everything they want when they want it. We all know this does not work.

With a purpose established, society would begin to see that concepts such as environmental improvements are not only beneficial for souls today but for future souls. This, in turn, is good for souls today for, after all, they will benefit in the growth of an omnipotent, omnipresent, omniscient force in the sense that they will once again become that very force and anything in the future that benefits that force, benefits them.

Society already has a limited amount of resources at any point in time and therefore must learn to project into the future in order to best utilize its resources of today. Part of society's resources involves people, and victims of trauma are resources that can benefit others if allowed to heal properly. Recovering from grief, whether caused by a loss of a loved one, violence, loss of something important to the soul, involves letting go, accepting the fact that a loss took place and cannot be undone, and moving on.

Do not misunderstand, this does not mean that a soul should just forget it happened. It does imply that a soul needs to forgive, for it cannot begin to let go and move on until the soul has come to peace with itself. There is a difference between forgiving and forgetting. It does not imply that the soul should necessarily move on in the sense of no longer working within the perimeters of that loss. Quite the contrary. Many were the beneficial actions taken by victimized souls as they sought to help other souls avoid the same grief.

Some examples involve initiating, strengthening, or perpetuating organizations that aid particular victims, becoming involved to see that the same thing does not happen to others, or just finding a way to get on with one's journey.

Parenting is another example of letting go. Parenting means allowing your child to make mistakes and still accepting them. It means counseling, loving, assisting, mentoring, protecting one's child throughout his life, but recognizing that each aspect of parenting changes as the child grows. A parent needs to know when to pull back and let the child stand alone. It means knowing when to begin letting go and when to finally let go.

Letting go for parents does not mean turning your back, rejecting, using your child for your own needs, molding your child into what you want. It means allowing your child to grow. Part of growing is making mistakes. It is at the times of making mistakes that children in our society need support, comfort, and mentoring. This is a time to let go of the child's mistake and move on with the child. Parents need to find a way to teach the children how to learn lessons from their mistakes. Punishment of a child should not be vindictive but rather instructional. It should center around the rights of souls and respect for journeys of souls.

What goes for the parent also goes for society. We all have a stake in children. They represent the future. Not just the future of this reality but the future growth of the force that created the very existence we occupy. An adult is no more than a child with additional learning experiences. Parents should not, just as punishment for a child should not, be vindictive, but rather instructive, as it should also be for adults, for all souls.

Letting go is a key component in life. Things don't happen to people as a punishment from above. Once one understands the purpose of one's soul, one begins to see that society, government, environmental concerns, social dilemmas, future goals, mankind, social programs, all take on a different light. They begin to take on a purpose: the purpose of assisting, not directing, souls. The purpose of assisting souls should be productive, be unobstructed, and be successful in the quest to fulfill the purpose for which they were sent.

Victims are souls that have been wounded in their journey in life. Victims all have one thing in common, a loss of some type. Victims all have to find a way of letting go. "The philosophy", a universal philosophy of some type, would help all victims let go. It would help them find peace by knowing that each and every soul has a purpose. It would help knowing that having lived and experienced life is that purpose. An injured soul must be set free. A universal philosophy can do that.

Letting Go / Forgiving

You Do Not Need To Punish Men

"In Summary"

We May Be God, But We Are Still Human

Society Ignores The Compassionate

In Our Society: Victim Once, Victim Twice

The Ripple Effect Applies To Those Responsible For Society

Society Must Ease The Victim's Burden

Society's Job Is To Protect The Journeys Of Souls

A Universal Philosophy Can Help

"Example is the school of mankind, and they will learn at no other."

Edmund Burke
(1729 – 1797)
Letters on a Regicide Peace

Chapter 25:
Missionary Work/Helping Others
♦
Everybody is a Missionary, Like it or Not

Missionary work is of utmost importance in our society. "The philosophy" does nothing to diminish the importance of this work. Quite the contrary; "the philosophy" accentuates the magnitude of the importance of missionary work and expands its scope to becoming a constant thought in man's mind. The problem is there are not enough missionaries and the number is rapidly shrinking in size and this is taking a great toll on our society, but let's tackle that concept after some reflection regarding what missionary work is.

Missionary work is conducted by everyone in society. In fact, everyone's life is a statement of missionary work regardless of their particular religion. Missionaries are people who undertake a mission and, in most contexts, this means a religious mission. A soul, your soul, my soul, is just passing through life. We either have a mission, a purpose in life, or nothing has a purpose. The purpose in life is directly related to religious concepts: the creator, birth, death, afterlife, experiencing life, all are religious experiences.

We have no choice but to experience life. It may be in a self or socially perceived positive manner or negative manner, but experience it we will. The time span may be "too short or too long", but in reality, the time span is relatively the same for all.

But how does missionary work come into play, how does it remain relevant, if "the philosophy" professes equality of all men, if "the philosophy" professes equality of all religions? If we are in fact all, each and every one of us, a piece of God, then each of us is a living testament to others of who God is. If we are here in an amnesiac state, on leave from God, then we need to pitch in together and assist each other. We, each of us, need to become a reinforcement mechanism, a pillar of strength, a missionary to others.

Life is tough and isn't getting any easier. One reason for the difficulties in life is due to people forgetting they are missionaries. They look at missionaries as people who dedicate their lives to God and go to a foreign country in order to spread their own particular religion with the hopes of saving souls.

Saving souls from "what" is the question. Saving souls from hell is the answer. But souls are God and we are God, so in essence we are saving God from hell while at the same time saving ourselves from the hell of the ripple effect. The ripple effect is but the realization, the true empathizing of how one's actions affected or did not affect others. A true and total empathizing of how they in turn affected or did not affect others due to our actions.

But if man's souls is actually a piece of God and goes back to God, why would He allow a soul, why would He allow Himself to suffer for eternity through the process of the ripple effect? How else is the Omnipotent, Omnipresent, Omnipotent

God to learn other than through creating, living, immersing Himself, ourselves, in experiences.

God cannot grow by staying within Himself. So He creates voids within Himself through which He can learn by living, creating, and immersing Himself with experiences. He interjects Himself into these voids. We are He and He is us. We are here for a reason. We have a sense of that reason, a deja vu regarding it.

With a sense of this in mind, the question once again surfaces, "Is missionary work necessary?" The question is one that appears natural to ask only because we have departed as a race so far from our purpose in life. We have lost track of who we are, and the concept of a purpose in life. Life seems to be just that: "life". But it is more than that; life as we know it is God in His purity, God in His infancy, God attempting to grow, for without growth there is only stagnation followed inevitably by a withering away of God's very own essence, our own essence, through the process of gradual dementia.

One cannot constantly refer to the Creative force as God. One must at some point recognize that when we refer to God, we are actually referring to ourselves, our own souls, since they are in essence a piece of God Himself infused into this reality we know. Therefore, a growing God is to our benefit. In a sense, one could say that the most selfish form of hedonism is the form of hedonism directed to self pleasure in the "afterlife". A form of life commitment oriented around pleasurable experiences other than negative experiences through the ripple effect once returning from whence we came.

One must therefore realize that to perform, participate in, or instigate deeds, actions, thoughts, or feelings that are beneficial to man and mankind is in truth self-serving. Although this is nothing but a form of hedonism, it is also a form of missionary work. On the other hand, one must also realize that this form of action, action directed at improving the lot of mankind, is not just self-serving for the self, but self-serving for the whole, in essence, all souls in the universe, man or otherwise.

Missionary work is a noble journey for the soul, but it, like mankind, is also in its infancy. It has much maturing to do. It too has lacked a true understanding of its purpose just as man has. Missionary work also has been asking, "Why?", "What's the purpose?" It too lacks an understanding of a total philosophy. Missionary work, like man, has relied entirely upon faith, devotion, a strong internal drive, a universal deja vu contained within all men in its past and now needs the strengthening of its foundation through the understanding of its purpose.

Why or how has it come about that man seems to be having such a tough time fighting the time eternal struggle of "good and evil"? Much of it has to do with the growth of mans' world. The expansion of knowledge in the fields of math, science, religion, philosophy, social skills, the expansion of communications technology, and population density, all have contributed to a horrendous data conflicting sensory overload of the minds of men. An overload so severe it has thrown men into a state of self-doubt in terms of the validity of their very selves, of their personal convictions.

The overload has become so overpowering that many men today have not just been thrown into self-doubt but have, in fact, cast aside their personal convictions and, what is truly sad, replaced their self-convictions with nothing except what is convenient at any particular time for a particular situation. Men are losing their principles. This concept is causing a major impact, a major problem within society today. It may be the major problem our society faces, not only today, but well into the future, unless we change our perceptions of ourselves, of man himself.

Mankind has not been able to add to his experiences the connecting concepts that will reinforce fields that he has developed over the course of his evolutionary progress. Man now has more than one field in which he has faith. These fields: math, science, religion, philosophy, universal mythology, and deja vu are all competing against each other in what they perceive to be a struggle for survival. If these fields of math, science, religion, philosophy, universal mythology, and deja vu, fields which man has carried with him since the beginning of time, cannot get along together, how can they expect men to get along with other men?

And these fields will never get along together until they realize they each have an extremely important part to play in mans' future development. This, in turn, can only come about through the development of a universal philosophy that provides the recognition of the importance of each through the incorporation of each into "the philosophy" itself. A universal philosophy that will show each the importance of its place in the future of man, the entity they have been accompanying throughout history.

Unfortunately, this lack of a total philosophy has lead to many horrendously inhumane acts in the name of the zealous beliefs religion, science, and philosophy profess. The massacres, tortures, demeaning actions, wars, and intimidation that has gone on in the hope of securing a personal place in heaven will truly be one of man's most illogical, shameful, disgusting behaviors to be chronicled in the annals of mans' history. On the other hand, history will have to make note that man did, in fact, lack a universal philosophy. Man did not have the knowledge, the communications, the global view needed to develop such a philosophy.

Each arena of man has been struggling to survive. Science, mathematics, religion, universal mythological concepts, mans' deja vu, pure philosophy, all have been struggling. All have been struggling against each other due to the erroneous impression that each is threatening the very existence of the other when in fact all are of vital importance to the thing mankind needs most: a universal philosophy. A universal philosophy will lead man, will lead mankind, to an understanding of just who he is, what his purpose is in this reality, how he is tied to other men, how he must perceive himself in relationship to other beings here on earth or, for that matter, someplace else in the universe.

This again leads us back to the question, "Is missionary work necessary?" There is so much to say about this, there is so little space to say it in. So let's start by saying, "There is nothing conflicting with the concept of missionary work and "the philosophy". It fits "the philosophy" beautifully. Missionary work, whether through "missionaries" or missionaries such as ministers, rabbis, priests, or institutions of religion, have been driven by self righteousness. What is wrong, with the past and present concept of missionary work, is the manner in which it has been approached in the past and to a large extent is still approached today.

The problem generated has been through the small minded approach that the missionary had "the" answer and everyone else was using faulty logic. Or the missionary held the belief that he represented an organization that had the one and only answer. This caused each to compete with the other. Each to attempt to dominate in order to keep itself from becoming extinct. A matter of survival of the fittest through the espousing of the brotherhood of all rather than through an understanding of true connection, via the souls of men, via God through the soul.

Once again, the paradox of man surfaces through the irrationality of mans' logic in the conception that only two people are ever right, himself and the man who agrees with him. So the Muslims were right and the Christians were wrong. The Christians were righteous and the Jews were lost souls. The Jews had the history and therefore others were misguided, etc., etc., etc.

"The philosophy", on the other hand, says they are all right. They each provide, in essence, the same universal teachings regarding the way man should live, regarding the way men should treat each other, regarding the value of a man, a soul. With the understanding of "the philosophy", science, mathematics, religion, universal mythological concepts, mans' deja vu, pure philosophy, all can become invaluable cooperative, universal tools, once again for man and men.

With the understanding of a universal philosophy, men, all men, will be able to add a universal foundation to their religions. A foundation of understanding, a means of unifying all men through the understanding of who we are, through the understanding that we do have a purpose, and through the understanding of just what that purpose is. This, in turn, may lead to a reversal of the mass exodus of missionaries within society. The concept that each and every man performs missionary work throughout his whole life is losing its recognition of significance. The individual missionary is becoming a lonely figure indeed.

People profess their beliefs in the institutions of their faiths, but leave those very institutions behind once immersed in their personal daily routines. They become worn, weary, beaten down souls unable to cope with the myriad of life's inundating, compromising, self-serving, egocentric situations through which they must muddle on a daily basis. They become confused through the constant observance and experiencing of actions of others that run contrary to their convictions and beliefs.

The souls in society are not connecting, are in fact becoming fragmentized, race against race, nationality against nationality, gender against gender. The population density and communications technology explosion have inundated individuals to such an extent that they find following their personal beliefs difficult to live in a consistent fashion. More and more pillars of society are falling through the erosion actions of the swirling waters of intolerant, biased, insensitive social behaviors. The collapse of a few pillars in society puts more weight upon the remaining pillars. The stress increases and more pillars fall. So the process goes, so the process accelerates. All of it becomes magnified and glorified by the media in an ever accelerating drive to be the largest draw of an audience at any cost. The more erosion that takes place, the faster it erodes.

We, men, need a means of coalescing our competing, fractionalized, internal drives of religious beliefs, philosophies, and search for knowledge. We need a foundation to our drives. We need a universal philosophy that will lead to tolerance and assistance of man to man, society to man, science to man, philosophy to man, and religion to man. What is forgotten is that we each make a statement to others every day, every hour, every minute. Each action we take or just as significantly, don't take, is a missionary statement.

We must all, once again, recognize that we are each missionaries in life. We must all understand that we each have a purpose in life. We must understand that we are all brothers in the soul, we are all a piece of God Himself.

We must all recognize that we are, each and everyone of us, missionaries, like it or not.

Missionary Work / Helping Others

Everybody Is A Missionary

"In Summary"

We Are Connected To Religion Through Life

Religious People Are Hedonists

Missionaries Aren't Just People In Foreign Countries

Mankind, Men, Are On Sensory Overload

Modern Communications Technology Ravages Mankind

Communications Technology Provides A Global View

Erosions Of The Pillars Of Society

Will The Roof Collapse?

You May Be "The" Essential Pillar Remaining

In Summary:
Intolerance Is An Outmoded Term
♦
Social Dilemmas Are Not Dilemmas

Social dilemmas appear to exist all around us. They reach into our past, distort our present, and add a twist of despair to our future. They sound so negative when put this way. They are negative to journeys of the souls. They are expectations of a society espousing individuality while chaining up the self expressions of, not only the masses, but the individual. They are expressions by society of tolerance while vividly portraying hostile, condemning, demeaning intolerance toward individuals and institutions that are clearly different.

They are the forked tongue of man, the verbalizing one belief and conviction while practicing another. And it is not one race, gender, economic status, class status, age group, or occupation that immerses itself in moral and verbal contradictions. It is all of them. It is the verbalization of the importance of the individual soul and the practice of intolerance for anything different than oneself or for one's beliefs. It is the very professing of men and institutions of the wonderful qualities of uniqueness as they are in the process of taking actions to make sure anyone different than they are, is held in check socially, legally, ethically.

Man, religions, and society have long professed tolerance, but they have never seemed to jump the hurdle of verbalizing and believing strongly enough in it to make it a true building block, a true foundation upon which to rest their structures of belief. Whenever some form of eccentricity surfaces that challenges the establishments, that challenges the beliefs of individuals, they almost always collapse the principle of the beauty of uniqueness and fall back to contain the apparent threat through outright violence, intimidation, isolation, withdrawal, domination, and the almighty argument, "I believe this or that because of faith and, therefore, I know I'm right and you are wrong. Therefore, you better believe what I tell you or you're out of here, literally."

Unfortunately for some people, they cannot verbalize their agreement to the intimidator because the point of contention is not composed of mental thoughts such as religious beliefs, political leanings, philosophical rationale, or any other types of mental exercises conducted within the privacy of one's skull. These people are of a different color, such as blacks in a white or yellow society. Whites within a black or yellow society or yellows within a black or white society. No one race has an exclusive on intolerance. They are people who have different sexual leanings and perceptions. Ones that do not fit the norm of what certain sections of society say should be "the" way. Norms that are felt by many and expected of others when, in fact, their bodies say otherwise. These are intolerances that are prolific and heated with little sensitivity to the soul of the "different" person. Even when the so-called deviant souls are not acting in any manner so as to adversely affect the journey of any other soul, society admonishes, demeans, and intimidates them. Society never seems to be able to stop trying to "cure" them. To society, this means making them feel or act like society feels they should feel or act, or in other words destroying their very uniqueness of individuality.

They are people with specific genders. They are the females of society; subjugated, used, squelched, blaming their woes upon the intolerance of the opposite gender. They are the males of society; shackled to the grindstone of work, subjugated, and used, blaming all their woes upon the intolerance of the opposite gender. The intolerance sometimes takes the form of status, ridicule, and belittlement: the rich against the poor, the poor against the rich, the prominent occupations over the less glorified jobs (even the names "job" and "occupation" express this), the job holders against the professionals, the people who live here as compared to there, and on and on it goes.

Even religions, which profess to have tolerance, get into the act: Catholics against the Muslims, Protestants against the Atheist, and the Atheist against everyone. Everyone thinks he is right and competes against the other constantly trying to expand their turf and protecting their territory out of fear, out of ignorance.

The reason: lack of tolerance for individual souls, lack of respect. Both respect and tolerance are espoused by nearly everyone and nearly all institutions but both are turned away from when any sensed threat of encroachment occurs, either real or imagined. Considering that man has a vivid imagination, this occurs very, very frequently. The result: little actual tolerance within our society. Better now than in the past? Yes, but still we haven't quite found a way to jump this hurdle of contradiction regarding what we profess and what our actions say we mean.

We have a working knowledge of the importance of tolerance. We have a subconscious sense of the significance of it. We even have a deja vu of the relevance of the purpose for the unique journeys of all souls made possible by the uniqueness of each machine. Yet we cannot quite implement the actual policies, behaviors, and private conversations that would display our true acceptance of tolerance of the importance of individuality.

Why? What's the hold up? We have had all forms of our institutions and a myriad of individuals throughout history working to establish the concept of tolerance and implant it once and for all with the rest of the universal principles of mankind. But all have failed to make the concept believable. Since these institutions are created by man, perhaps they are missing the same answers individuals are missing. Perhaps they cannot come to grips with the concept of tolerance and truly implement it until that answer is found. Perhaps the answer to who we are, where we came from before this reality, what our purpose is in this reality, and where we are headed after this reality would help us understand. And understanding would definitely help us know if our professed convictions are on the right track. Knowing this could then lead us from the verbalization to modeling through action.

What's missing is a universal philosophy that will lead all men, all institutions, into recognizing not only their personal significance but also the significance of all souls in relationship to each other and, even more importantly, in our return to our next reality. All this brings us right back to the beginning of our discourse: social dilemmas. It appears that social dilemmas are man-made. They are illogical actions going against the grain of what we as men profess verbally and sense from the depths of our souls.

Social dilemmas are not dilemmas; they are a fabrication of man and man's institutions used to protect turf, used to protect ourselves from probing and thought-provoking concepts that we sense may shake our faiths, our principles, our own identity of who we are. The elimination of social dilemmas will only come about when we as souls, as men, recognize the significance of our own souls. Once we attain this understanding, we will be able to accept ourselves for who we are, individuals, unique in our own significance. Once we have gained confidence in our own self worth, we will no longer need to fear others shaking our personal beliefs which we carry with us as we journey though life. Through the knowledge that we are all unique and understanding, why it is important to remain so, we will be able to accept, not only in thought, but in actions, the fact that the same applies to others also.

When this happens we can begin to reform our approach to people, to souls. We can begin to reanalyze our society and reform it to fit our concept of who we are and what our journey as men is, rather than engineer society in a manner intended to dominate others in order to preserve our own beliefs and identities.

To get to somewhere we have never been able to get to before will take some special thought. It will take a cooperative effort. It will take people opening their minds to new ideas. Ideas that will not compromise the basics of your beliefs but may trim some of the intolerance. Respect for traditions established down through the history of man, respect for the uniqueness of souls, respect for the wide variety of homes for the soul: religions, all are a must. We need to respect tolerance, the uniqueness of the souls, the importance of institutions as well as souls to be unique. We must guard not only their own uniqueness but the uniqueness of other souls and institutions of souls.

Churches, mosques, synagogues, and holy places emanate the creative abilities of God Himself. They should be places men, souls, can seek shelter and use as homes, as shelters, in which to seek refuge in their difficult journeys regardless of their differences. They are places where all men should show respect for each other and feel a commonality of purpose, a brotherhood of the soul. These are places where men should be able to focus their beliefs, teachings, history, traditions, and commitments into a single point of contemplation and acute awareness that is so intense that it reaches into the depths of his very soul. These institutions are locations where men should be able to feel their connection to God within Himself.

What about man sensing God outside Himself? Where should all men be able to feel the connection of his physical self to God? Where should he be able to literally feel his skin prickle with electricity as he makes the connection? It is the most sacred place of all. It is outside the institutions of religion.

Religions are homes for the soul. Society is home for the machine. It is in society itself where souls reconfirm their faith in each other, strengthen their brotherhood of souls. The soul meditates in the religious institutions. One's actions there are on an exemplary level since one is surrounded by one's personal convictions. In society, however, the soul no longer is surrounded with constant reminders. It is here where the strength of one's personal convictions show. It is in society where men come into contact with man the human. Society is where men expose their true convictions and stand as pillars of strength for society.

It is time we, as men, examine our beliefs. It is time we coalesce the knowledge we have, and intuition we sense, and build a foundation to our present beliefs that will allow us to literally accept the philosophies we espouse. A foundation so strong it will allow us to build upon our individuality, take pride in its existence, and jealously guard its right for survival, not only for our own soul, but for everyone's soul.

It's time we develop a universal philosophy. It's time we bring down the man-made walls of social dilemmas in order to let all men become a part of mans' quest. There is more than enough work for all of us. We need everyone's help in our journey through life, in our journey into the starts, in the personal journeys that will complete the circle for each of us, a reinfusion back into the essence of God Himself.

"In Summary"

Intolerance Creates Social Dilemmas

Society Does Not Tolerate Uniqueness Well

Race, Religion, Genders Are Unique In Their Own Way

Social Dilemmas Are Fabricated By Man

Society Is Home For The Machine

Religions Are Homes For Souls

It Is Time To Bring Down The Wall Of Social Dilemmas

It Is Time For A Universal Philosophy

It Is Time To Recognize Our Beginning Is Our End

A Circle Completed

Part C.

Man

Historical Reflections

C. MAN
Historical Reflections and the Future......302

Introduction
Predestination/Free Will, Both at the Same Time.....305

27. **God/gods**
   A Name Does Not Make God................315
28. **Good/Bad**
   No such Thing as Good and Bad..........327
29. **Heaven/Hell**
   Some Things are Worth Repeating.........333
30. **God is Going to Get You for That**
   God has no need to Inflict Vengeance Upon Himself....................341
31. **Christianity/Religions**
   All are One.................351
32. **Jesus Christ/"the Philosophy"**
   There is noConflict...............361

33. **In Summary**
   History is Meant to Guide One Into the Future...................367

THE BOOK IN SUMMARY
Two Statements/Nine Words................377

A Special Page of Thanks.................380
Addendum: To My Students...............381
Suggested Reading List.................386
About the Author.................387

Introduction: Predestination/Free Will Both At The Same Time

♦

It's Time To "Think Out Of The Box"

Predestination and free will: one or the other seems to be the case as man speculates through his philosophical reflections. The two seem to be at odds with one another. When one begins to speculate about man and how he might fit into the puzzle of eternity, the concepts begin to change. As a universal philosophy develops by adding bits and pieces of science, philosophy, religion, mysticism, mythology, and deja vu together, surprising concepts can emerge.

Universal philosophies will force one to reexamine the fringes of various fields, trim off the excesses, retain the substance, and cherish the traditions as enrichment and coloring for the basic foundations. "The philosophy" does just that type of thing. "The philosophy" speculates in terms of a total picture of man. It attempts to add a foundation to the historical institutions of man. It attempts to act as a cementing agent, as a foundation to man's search for truths.

If we use "the philosophy" as described in Book I, then we can accept predestination as relevant in understanding that our being placed within this reality was a predetermined action. An action that was derived out of necessity not just for the growth but for the very existence of the Creator of our reality. So we were predestined to come into this reality.

We were extracted from God, by God, and sent here as a piece of God. We were placed within this reality to serve a purpose.

This was done as a means by which an omnipotent, omniscient, omnipresent force could become even more so. But in order to be creative, experience new things, and gain new insights, we had to be placed here in an amnesiac state or else we would only be able to think within the confines of our omnipotent power, knowledge, and presence. We would never be able to "think out of the box".

The bottom line, we were knowingly and intentionally placed here by ourselves, by God – that was predestined. We are amnesiac to the fact – that was predestined. We will return – that was predestined. We came into this world naked physically and mentally – that was predestined. And we will return draped in experiences, insights, knowledge, awareness, of all that we did and did not do – that is predestined. As we return to God and become God once again, we will be made fully aware, in every sense conceivable, of the events for which we were responsible and the ripple effect generated from those events – that is predestined. A ripple effect that will go into eternity itself. An eternity that will outlast the very universe, the very reality we know as man.

The eventual annihilation of our reality will not mean the annihilation of God, for it was a creation of God. The destruction of our universe will not lead to the destruction of you or I since we are all a piece of God and become infused back into Him after our journey within this reality. But if that is true, then the actions we take within this reality and the effects it has through the ripple effect will never be forgotten for it will become a part of God Himself through us. And since we will then be a part of God, we will forever be aware of what actions we have taken and what the resultant ripple effects were, that is predestined.

The concept "forever" is significant here, for it doesn't mean until the end of the universe. It means forever. It doesn't mean until the end of time, for time is only relevant within the confines of the reality of our universe. So forever being aware of our action and how it, in turn, affected "forever" is a predestined culmination of man and mans' purpose. An awareness into forever and of a magnitude in scope so all-encompassing that the magnitude of its significance is equal to the magnitude of God Himself. And you are responsible for it. You are in control of it. You have "free will".

We cannot control the previously predestined events. They are predestined. But we can control what we do while we are within this reality. Knowing about the ripple effect, understanding it and how we fit into the concept of reality, can give us a great deal of insight as to how we as individuals want to proceed within this reality. We were sent here for a reason. We were sent into this reality to experience, create, and gain new insights. We were sent here to expand the very omniscience, omnipotence, and omnipresence of God Himself, of ourselves. Understanding that reason, that purpose, will help us determine the paths we wish to follow as we travel through this reality.

God put us here with free will so we could create, experience new things, and gain new insights. If we just remained within God Himself, we would never be able to generate "new" anything since we would know all there is to know and experience.

So here we sit with free will, wondering what to do. Well, we should be doing the same things religions have been suggesting to us for thousands of years. Religions are guidelines for us, for our souls. Religions have constantly been telling us to take a certain path in life or else God will punish you. Well, God is not going to get you for that. He doesn't need to. Your being "forever" aware in every sense of the word of your actions and the ripple effect they had, being "aware" into "forever" thus affecting "forever" into eternity itself, will be as much of a punishment and reward any soul could bear or hope to acquire.

Knowing this leads one to reflect upon many temptations. It causes one to think twice before taking any actions. It causes one to reevaluate one's perception of what is of value and what isn't, what is important and what isn't, what is significant and what isn't. It leads one to realize that he is contained and refrained by his humanly limitations. It leads one to accept himself as human and take refuge in the words: I am only human. But don't forget, you may be only human, but you roam this reality with free will and no one but you will be responsible for your actions when you exit this reality.

Free will means control over one's journey through this reality. It doesn't mean we control the building of the machine we occupy, nor does it mean we can always control it. If a soul enters a machine, a mind and body it cannot control, the other souls in control of their machines must assist in getting the renegade machine controlled. In some cases, it may mean providing specific instructions regarding patterns of behavior to follow. In other cases, it may mean direct supervision. And in other cases, it may mean actual confinement. In all cases, however, it must be recognized that there is a soul within the machine, a fellow soul, one with which we will one day again be reunited in the true sense of the word.

In no case can we abuse that soul through the abuse of the machine it occupies. The machine is not sacred, but the soul within is. On the other hand, we have a responsibility to our own soul and the souls of others to make this reality a safe, productive environment within which these very souls are to journey. Therefore, we each have an obligation to help restrain souls that interfere with journeys of other souls, to be sure they do not further interfere with the journey of others.

This then leads us into free will and the consequences it has upon the way we perceive our actions as individuals and as a society with regards to ourselves and others. It helps put religious concepts into perspective and gain a better acceptance and tolerance toward our fellow souls.

The concept of drugs takes on a different light. Now the responsibilities for one's actions comes home to the individual instead of society. We are all responsible for our own actions and the blame for our actions cannot be placed upon someone else's shoulders just because we do not want to suffer the consequences. We will feel the repercussion of becoming a heroine addict, not only because it hurt us, but because of the harm it brings to one's children, parents, friends, associates, spouses and people in society.

Becoming an addict is not necessarily a bad thing. Coffee drinkers are not a bad influence upon society. Cigarette smokers are not a bad influence compared to cocaine addicts. The influence of addiction is relative to the degree it hampers one's journey within reality. Influence here applies to how the action affects others but also how it affects yourself – for if your journey is affected, that changes how you in turn might have affected the journey of another soul.

Unfortunately, society often sticks its nose into the business of the journeys of individual souls. It places inappropriate restrictions upon those journeys in a good-intentioned manner that often has the reverse affect. Drug use is one such case. By outlawing drugs, society compounds the problems of the addict in terms of his repercussions in the afterlife. Outlawing drugs isn't done in the context of doing what's best for a particular soul's journey, but rather with the self righteous determination to impose one's own morals upon others in a power play of grand showmanship.

It's estimated that as much as 80% of the present prison population is vegetating in jail due to some connection with drugs. Keep in mind that in many of these cases, we are not protecting society from the individual but rather attempting to protect the individual from himself. We are trying to protect him from his own journey for which he himself will be held accountable through the ripple effect. We are placing more pressures on families, friends, neighbors, and even races. Pressures that will affect their very journeys through reality. Affects for which we will be held accountable through our own ripple effects.

Should people be allowed to obtain drugs within our society? It's their life. It's their journey. It will be their responsibility to face. Sure we would like to see that they do not, as we see it, waste their lives, but you have no right to decide what journey a person decides to take in his reality. You have the right to assist him, to provide protection for him from other souls, but you do not have the right to force his soul to do what you think his soul should do.

Should we allow people to sell drugs to people? That's a different situation. Many of these people are getting people involved for their own gain. They are adversely influencing the journey of souls for their own self interests. This is an example of an uncontrolled machine. A machine that needs to be restrained in some fashion from continuing to repeat his actions.

Drugs aren't the only concept that would require a reexamination. There are countless laws, social taboos, religious doctrines, etc., that would need to be examined in terms of man not being man but rather a traveler in time occupying a machine. A traveler with a purpose. A traveler who is in actuality God Himself.

We might have to start asking ourselves, "Would it be reasonable for me to expect God to obey that law, believe that doctrine, or resist that taboo?" If you were going to place restrictions upon God Himself, then there had better be a mighty good rationale for it. The same goes for your fellow man. Man is not the physical body, he is the soul within. He is God. He is here for a purpose. He was sent here by God Himself to journey through this reality, and if you are going to interfere with his journey you had better have a mighty good rationale for doing so, for in essence you are interfering with the journey of God Himself.

Man has free will. Man was given free will for a purpose. Man was sent to journey through this reality. No one has the right to interfere with that journey unless it is endangering or interfering with the free will and journey of other souls.

Predestination / Free Will

Both At The Same Time

"In Summary"

A Universal Philosophy Generates Surprising Concepts

We Were Predestined To Enter Reality

We Have A Purpose In Reality

Annihilation Of Our Reality Would Not Diminish The Results Of Our Existence In Reality

Once Placed In Reality, We Have Free Will

Without Free Will, Your Soul Is But A Machine

Free Will Gives Us Control Over Our Journey Through Reality

Being Given Free Will Means Being Responsible For Your Journey

"What's in a name? That which we call a rose by any other name would smell as sweet."

William Shakespeare (1564 – 1616)
A Midsummer-Night's Dream, Act II

Chapter 27:
God/gods
♦
A Name Does Not Make God

God, Zeus, Allah, Jehovah, The Great Spirit in the Sky, who cares? And for those who do, how petty. What *is* is, what was *was*, and what will be *will be* and there is nothing, creatures as impotent as we, can do about it other than accept our place in the scheme of things and attempt to serve our function as best we can and this is where we must begin to change. This is not a statement of despair nor a statement of resignation. Quite the contrary. It is a statement of elation and excitement in the recognition that we do actually have a purpose and a place in the scheme of things.

One of the things holding us back, however, is the notion that God is different than god, that each of us thinks our personal God is the right god, that each of our personal religions tend to believe that others are living in ignorance and need to be converted in order to find salvation.

This is the essence around which this book revolves. This book is an attempt at making a quantum leap in regards to our participation as individuals and a species to the big picture, the scheme of things, our purpose as man and men. This book is an attempt to establish our purpose and then determine just how we can improve our contribution in accomplishing this purpose.

Religions are important. They are the shelters for the traveling soul as it seeks to fulfill its purpose for which it was given its present state. Religions cannot be discarded nor can they be fractional, bickering, or divisive with regards to each other. They evolved in order to fill a niche needed by souls in their quest of fulfillment. They must aid each other, for the quest of the individual soul is long and tedious, filled with as much hardship and despair as hope and joy. It is religions that act as houses of refuge for the tired and weary soul. Religions must be preserved and encouraged for their purpose is significant and vital to the very soul itself.

God and gods – how can a religious individual internally reconcile the concept that gods and God are not important enough concepts to fight over? After all, man has been fighting over whose god is the true god for thousands of years. How can we give up this notion now, after all these years, and all this blood has been shed? After all, if we just gave up the notion that "our" god is the true god, would this not be sacrilegious in itself since so much suffering has taken place in the ages past to establish this "fact"?

It is time to stop bickering about whose god is the true god. It is time to "put away childish things" and move on to adolescence. It is time to grow into our individuality, our purpose in life, and our purpose in the overall scheme of reality, while at the same time growing into our acceptance of man as a whole man and as a social entity with a purpose of its own. It is time to gain tolerance towards all men. It is time to truly recognize all men as our brothers.

In order to accelerate the momentum of mankind in this direction, we must do two things.

First, we must examine our past and begin to accept the fact that our past actions have been a case of power plays to establish organizational dominance by large power groups in order to perpetuate their existence. Organizations have as compelling a desire to survive as individuals do. They have a life of their own and just as strong of a primordial instinct to survive as do individuals. But just as individuals have been wandering about in a disoriented state, lacking an understanding of their purpose in the scheme of life, these very same religious organizations have also been staggering about seeking out their true understanding of their function as to their purpose in reality.

Does this mean to imply that all the suffering, killing, atrocities, and guilt imposed upon people by religious organizations was in violation of man's, soul's, quest for fulfillment in its very purpose in life itself? Definitely. Does this mean our total history as a species has been for naught? By no means. We have come a long way as a species and have carried ourselves, albeit rather precariously, to the brink of a new age. We are standing on the edge of a new era, the era of mans' leap off this good earth and into the heavens. We are at the doorway of entering the very dream man has been striving for since the beginning of his existence.

Our journey to this point may be riddled with atrocities, but it has also been filled with many heroic stands and proud actions to which all men may look back upon with much pride and inspiration. We may have had much of our past blanketed with shameful acts, but each act will find its counterpart of good and compassionate victories over the dark deeds.

How appropriate that we should now be approaching the next gigantic leap of mankind, the leap off this very earth into the heavens, at the turn of the millennia. A coincidence? I suppose, if you believe in coincidences. The question is, will we be able to make this leap now at the dawning of this new millennia or might we have to wait for another thousand or two thousand years?

If we are to make the leap into the heavens at this dawning of the new millennia, just how do we wish to enter the very heavens themselves? Do we wish to enter the heavens as a species fighting, bickering, and committing atrocities amongst and to each other, or do we wish to enter the heavens as a peaceful cooperative species attempting to be a positive factor in the heavens? If we enter the heavens as a bickering, greedy, self serving species, we may very well indeed be bringing an infectious element into the heavens, much as we did once before in our past when we literally carried infectious diseases into the "new world", which in turn lead to the decimation of many cultures and populations. The old concept still holds true that those who don't study history are doomed to repeat it and the sad thing is that many innocent beings will suffer in the process.

Second, we must open our hearts up to the fact that our past personal beliefs of "our" god being the "true" god is not a "fact". It just is. Everyone's god is God, for by definition, God is the creator of the Universe. This is a simple but profound definition. It is not a statement that God is our creator. It is that God is the Creator of the Universe – our Universe.

The definition did not state that God is the creator of mankind, although if He created the universe and if we are a part of the creation of the universe, then He created us. So many variations and possibilities exist here, but they all lead to the same conclusion in the end.

Some creative ideas of man have no earthshaking consequences even if they proved to be true. For instance, if mankind were found to be the result of a penal institution by an extraterrestial life form, if mankind were found to be the result of gene implantation through artificial or biological means into a primitive life form already established upon this earth, if man should be found to be truly evolutionary in nature as the evolutionists contend, or if man should be found to be the direct result of the Creator, makes no difference. All the bickering over these concepts, the mental, emotional, and physical intimidation and coercion that has been wrought in the past to establish a dominance of a particular belief, is for naught. Whatever is, is and we will never be able to change the fact, whatever we finally find the truth to be. In all cases, however, the same fact will evolve; whoever or whatever caused the initial step that lead to our existence, may or may not be God.

Three possibilities exist where our God is the creator of our universe and one exists where our God is not the creator of the universe.

If the initial step which lead to our existence was an intelligent life form that already existed in our universe, then that life form would not be God. We would then have just been a creation of the creator that created us as a species. This would not alter the concept that our very essence, our souls, are still nothing less than a piece of God, the creator of our universe, Himself.

If the initial step which lead to our existence was the molding of clay by the Creator of the universe itself, then again it would not alter the concept that our very essence, our souls, were still nothing less than a piece of God Himself.

If the initial step which lead to our existence was found to be nothing other than a piece of God, Himself, wrenched from his very existence, then again it would not alter the concept that the very essence of our souls is still nothing less than a piece of God Himself.

And finally, if the initial step which leads to our existence was found to be a preexisting condition of our existence, independent of and in conjunction with the creator of the universe as we perceive it, then it would not alter the concept that our very essence, our souls, is still nothing less than an equal of God Himself, and thus still God Himself.

In each of these four cases, nothing has changed. In each of these cases we would still be shouldered with the fact that there is a purpose. Nothing, so complex yet so simple, so immense yet so small, so structured, yet so chaotic as our universe and our existence, could have just happened. It had to be planned and planned for a reason. Since we are a part of it, we had to be planned for a reason. What other reason could be given, than that explained in part I of this book – the philosophy?

In all cases, however, nothing alters the fact that we have a purpose, since by definition, if we do not have a purpose, then we do not have a purpose, and thus, things that happen have no significance. Therefore, we have only one significant philosophy to follow in the end, and that is that we have a purpose. We must then find our purpose in order to give our historical foundations a foundation of their own. This will provide what man has been seeking throughout history, an understanding of the general purpose of each individual and this in turn will result in the understanding that we are all truly brothers and thus all equally important. Finally, we will understand that tolerance of one individual towards another is not a pleasantry but an absolute necessity.

An analogy might go as follows: a biological mother (god) gives up his child for adoption. The child is never told directly of the history (insertion of the soul into the universe in an amnesiatic state). Over the next fifty years, the child senses something is not all it is perceived to be (deja vu, intuition, faith, etc.). The child searches for his past due to his sense of unease and inner sense of being driven to find some unknown information (spiritual, scientific, and unexplainable inner drives). The child finds enough information (religious, intuitive, and scientific) to draw a rational and accurate conclusion to his origin, his biological mother (from whence his soul originates). Not wishing to reject his nurturing mother (religious faiths) that has provided him with shelter and comfort over the years (faith, forgiveness, and guidance), he rejects the truth of his origin (he is actually a piece of God and therefore God Himself). He finds it comforting to huddle in the arms of his nurturing mother (religion) but at the same time is aware of the fact that new information is continually surfacing regarding his actual history. How will the analogy end? Who knows. It has two possible endings.

In one case, man rejects his biological mother and continues in the same path he has been taking for thousands of years. A path of turmoil, rejection of the individual's worth, attempts at dominance of one individual or organization over another through force, guilt, coercion, subjugation, and greed. This would be a path that will either prevent him from making his leap into the heavens, the leap he has yearned and strived for generations, or it will prove to be a path that will follow him into the heavens to contaminate all he touches.

Or, in the other case, man can accept his biological mother (his purpose in life and his place in the scheme of things) and add its richness to the warmth and comfort of his nurturing mother. In this case, he will finally come to peace with himself and accept himself for who he is. Thus eliminating much of the strife and need for his inhumane historical behavior and allow for the next quantum leap as a positive, motivated, creative element to be added to the heavens themselves.

In either case, the biological mother (God) is still the biological mother and nothing the child does or wishes to believe will alter that fact. No matter how many times the child professes his belief (faith) in the concept that his nurturing mother (personal religion) is his true mother (true God) nothing will be able to alter the fact that his true biological mother (God) is his true biological mother (God). God or god, it doesn't matter for they are, in the end, all the same whether we wish to believe it or not. What will matter, however, is that without a true understanding of our purpose in life, of our reason for existence, we will not be able to finally resolve our differences since we will not recognize our true commonality as men, for our true commonality as men lies not in our physical origins but in the origins of our souls.

Without the acceptance of the commonality of the origin of all men's souls and the commonality of their purpose in life, men will never be able to eliminate racial, social, economic, ideological, religious, and petty strifes that have haunted him since the beginning of his existence in this universe. These human conflicts that have haunted him will never be resolved and put to rest until he finally resolves his age old haunting of just who he really is and what his purpose is in this reality in which he exists.

God / gods

A Name Does Not Make A God

"In Summary"

God Is God Regardless Of What We Call Him

All Religions Are Important

Our Past Will Be Our Future Unless We Change

Four Possibilities Of God Exist

Man Knows His Nurturing Mother

Man Needs To Accept His Biological Mother

All Men Have A Commonality Of Souls

Yes, We Are All Brothers

"One and the same thing can at the same time be good, bad, and indifferent, e.g. music is good to the melancholy, bad to those who mourn, and neither good nor bad to the deaf."

Benedict Spinoza (1632 – 1677)
Ethics Part IV, Preface (1677)

Chapter 28:
Good/Bad: Misnomers
♦
There Is No Such Thing As Good And Bad

The concept of good and bad has been with man since the beginning of time. It is a concept that has fulfilled its purpose but which now has become outdated and restrictive in our relatively intellectual societies and cultures. For some cultures and geographical regions on earth, it is still viable and has its purpose, however in most parts of the educated, industrially advanced, and technologically budding regions, it is not an asset. Rather, it is an untruth that acts in a restrictive, inhibiting, narrow minded, aggressively initiating manner.

How could the concept of good and bad be good at one point of mans' behavior and be bad at another point? Early in the history of man, we had no concept or understanding of our purpose in life or our function and place in the scheme of the universe. At this stage we needed a means of conceptualizing and verbalizing the idea of right and wrong, acceptable and unacceptable, black and white, moral and immoral. What better means to define this concept than through the religions of the world projecting pictures of good and bad, heaven and hell, sin and righteousness, God and the Devil. These concepts needed a strong position in our cultures in order to provide a guideline for men to follow.

The concepts of parallel universes, ripple effects, we are God, God is us, deja vu, creation of something from nothing, time has no meaning, etc., were concepts that could not be rationalized into our religions and logic. Science had not yet expanded its sphere of knowledge to the point where it actually overlapped portions of the spheres of religion and intuition. In other words, there were many missing links.

In the past the missing link had not been suggested, exposed, or philosophically sought out in a universal drive to coalesce mans' total historical reflections pertaining to philosophy and religion. As we begin to accept logical concepts such as: God can make a universe from nothing, we are a piece of God interjected into this universe in an amnesiac state for a purpose. Our purpose is to aid in the expansion of the omnipresent, omnipotent, and omniscient being, and we will return to our origin from which we came. Then the concept of good and bad will become irrelevant. We will begin to see that the concept of good and bad is not good or bad in the scheme of things but rather will play a very significant role in terms of what our individual soul will have to live with for eternity.

With this perspective, actions or inactions on an individual's or society's part no longer are good or bad but rather just is. For the Creative Force, the action or inaction will just add to the total knowledge available. The initiator and participant of the action or inaction, no matter how sure of their actions or direct involvement with the action, will live with the results and the ripple effect for eternity.

This then leads one to look at the concept of good and evil as a primitive concept to be replaced with a broader recognition that the concept of good and evil does nothing other than act as a blind guideline. Whereas the recognition of your purpose in life and place in the scheme of eternity causes one to reflect upon one's action not because it is good or bad but in terms of a broader more understandable insight. It begins to magnify the importance of the individual's actions to the individual as well as society and the species. It begins to cause one to realize the actions one takes, the manner in which one perceives the events that befall oneself, and the process of scrutinizing another person or their actions may in actuality have little significance. Rather, what has significance is taking care of one's own actions. Placing one's energy into taking responsibility of one's own behavior, and how one influences another in society through action or, just as importantly, inaction. One begins to realize that one will live for eternity, through the ripple effect, the results of all of one's existence in our present state. Thus actions or lack of action begins to transcend other worldly concepts such as materialism, vengeance, revenge, dominance, control, intimidation, greed, etc., etc.

Good and bad, is there such a thing? No; but ironically, we will all certainly think so when we complete our circle and return back to our individual points of origin.

You & I Together

Good / Bad

No Such Thing As Good And Bad

"In Summary"

Good And Bad Has Served Us Well

It's Time To Put Them To Rest And Move On

Sin Is Not Sin

Bad Is Not Bad

Good Is Not Good

The Devil Never Makes Anyone Do Anything

We Will Have To Take Responsibility For All Our Own Actions

We Will Not Be Able To Blame Anyone Else For What We've Done

> *"The grave is the first stage of the journey into eternity."*
>
> Mohammed (570 – 632)
> Prophet of Islam

Chapter 29: Heaven and Hell

♦

Some Things Are Worth Repeating

The crux of many religions. The concept that throws hope and fear into the minds of men. The concept that causes men to radiate with optimism and tremble with pessimism. The concept that has driven history since recorded time. Just what is heaven and what is hell and do they exist at all? If you can accept the facts that:

1. we or our souls originated as a piece of God from God

2. we are indeed a piece of God sent in an amnesiac state to work in a void in order to create unique ideas, since God in His omniscience cannot create new unique ideas due to the fact that He is omniscient

3. we will return to God and become a part of God again

4. and we will be conscious of our individual actions or inactions on Earth in order to relay them to God,

then yes, there is a heaven and a hell, and fortunately or unfortunately, we will all be condemned to heaven and hell both.

Let me explain. If we do go to another reality or consciousness after "death", we will be aware of all our individual actions. That is not as simple a concept as it appears on the surface. Awareness of all our individualistic actions means that literally. Even in our own reality of our present state of consciousness we are not aware of all the ramifications of our actions in terms of the true depth at which each of our actions affect people, their psyche, and their egos. We cannot begin to empathize with them regarding the internal series of events that our actions initiate within an individual.

What is even more staggering is the fact that we cannot even begin to understand, let alone comprehend, how each of our personal actions, leads to actions by the individuals at whom our actions were directed, to react to other individuals, which leads to actions affecting other individuals, which leads to actions affecting other individuals, etc. etc. ad infinitum. This is what is known as the ripple effect.

Being mere "mortals" we cannot begin to fully comprehend, understand, or empathize with these multiple ripple effect situations. We need not feel guilty about this considering our limited mental capacity and our limited emotional capabilities. We need, however, to listen to our inner voices, our religious teachings, and our historical lessons. They all act as a manual for us to show us the general paths we would be wise to follow, to show us that we are our Brother's Keeper. We are all truly brothers, if one accepts the concepts: we all have souls, souls are nothing but a piece of God, and that finally we will all return once again into the being from which we came, regardless of our color, sex, race, relative intelligence, or religion.

So where does heaven and hell come into the picture? If we

return to God and fuse into his essence, we become God again. If we become God again, we become omniscient again. If we are omniscient again, we will know everything, understand everything, and empathize with everything. The unsettling part of this then is that we will become truly aware of, understanding of, comprehending of, and empathetic of all the ways in which our actions as "mortals" affected not just others but how others affected others down the line etc., etc., due to the ripple effect of our actions.

Think about that. You will know and actually feel how each positive action you took towards other individuals directly or indirectly affected them and all the individuals that person in turn affected positively due to our actions etc., etc., forever and ever into "eternity." The taste, the glow, the satisfaction of the good a person initiates and its ripple effect would then live with them into "eternity." It would take a good deal of eternity for there would be an almost infinite number of direct and indirect repercussions generated from each positive action an individual takes. This would be what one would call heaven.

On the other hand, you will also know and actually feel how each negative action you took towards other individuals directly or indirectly affected them and all the individuals that person in turn affected negatively due to our actions etc., etc. forever and ever into "eternity." The anger, hate, jealousy, resentment, perversions, irritation, pain, sorrow, and despair a person initiates and its ripple effect would then live with them into "eternity." This in turn would take a good deal of eternity for there would be an almost infinite number of direct and indirect repercussions generated from each negative action an individual takes. This would then be what one would call hell. Heaven and Hell? Yes, a true heaven and hell for all of us, and for some of us more heaven and for others more hell.

Is there forgiveness in heaven? Yes, why not, for your total consciousness after death of your impact on others in the research lab of the universe will be yours to live with throughout eternity. This will not be intended as a punishment but rather just as a simple realization of your impact. You will have to live with your true understanding and empathizing for eternity with each of the direct and indirect repercussions created from the actions your soul initiates in this reality.

Every feeling of pain, of despair will live with you forever. No wonder men tremble with fear of hell even though they did not and do not understand it. How ironic the concept really is that we really are unwittingly creating our own hell. Even simple negative actions of a nasty stare and an intolerant blast of the horn will have their ripple effects which we will be fully aware of in all sense of the words forever and ever. Likewise every feeling of joy, love, and hope will live with you forever. No wonder men seek control of their mortal impulses and tendencies. No wonder men have looked to religions to help them see the "truth" and the "light." Even simplistic deeds of goodwill such as a "good morning", "may I help you", and a wave to let someone, who was confused, into a traffic space, will have their ripple effects which we will be fully aware of in all sense of the words forever and ever.

Heaven? Yes. Hell? Yes. Punishment? No. Vindictiveness? No. It just is what it is and we each will have nobody to blame but ourselves, for we are each responsible for our own actions as much as we might wish otherwise. There will be no excuses, no blaming society, no blaming economics, no blaming other people, just the realization that we all had free will and did with it what we did. Pure and simple.

Is there a Hell? Returning to an eternal afterlife relegated to be conscious of and empathetic of all the deep feelings we have initiated upon others and the subsequent ripple effects that never cease involving shame, pain, despair, desperation, depression, isolation, rejection, humiliation, fear, anger, hate, jealousy, loneliness, and rejection will be hell enough for any man to bear into eternity.

Is there a Heaven? Returning to an eternal afterlife relegated to be conscious of and empathetic of all the deep feelings we have initiated upon others and the subsequent ripple effects that never cease involving pride, delight, elation, love, affection, confidence, friendship, trust, inclusion, wonder, awe, appreciation, satisfaction, and delight will be heaven enough for any man to experience into eternity.

Heaven / Hell

Some Things Are Worth Repeating

"In Summary"

Heaven And Hell – The Crux Of Religions

Look Out For The Ripple Effect

Mere Mortals Cannot Fully Comprehend

Positive And Negative – You Will Know The Difference

More Heaven For Some, More Hell For Others

Heaven And Hell For All

God Does Not Need To Punish

Hell Is Not A Punishment, It Just Is

Vengeance is mine; I will repay, saith the Lord.
Romans 12:19

Chapter 30:
"God Is Going To Get You For That"
♦
God Has No Need To Inflict Vengeance Upon Himself

"God's going to get you for that." How often we think it. How often it has been either insinuated or directly spewed before us. It is so ingrained in mankind by religions that it is a global phenomenon: war, famine, plague, depression, disintegration of civilizations, earthquakes, monsoons, genocide, etc., etc. Frequently it is accompanied by the thought, "It didn't happen here because we have God on our side."

It surfaces in the consciousness of individuals when they begin to experience problems closer to home: AIDS, cancer, heart attacks, suicides, accidents, financial trouble, mental illness, sickness, abusive spouses, drug addiction, rape, physical and verbal assault, the list goes on and on. It is taught so universally that it even strikes into the very hearts of children. They not only sense it, but will verbalize it when they experience the effects of divorce, alcoholism, child abuse, death, job displacement, depression, sibling rivalry, and even failing a test or not being invited to a party.

"God's going to get you for that." What a dehumanizing, demeaning concept. Religions speak of "the Creator" of this reality as an all powerful, all knowing, all present force. A force that went on to create man as an entity within the reality. They then proceed to explain that this same Creator, the one that had the knowledge and power, the one that was so all prevalent that he was everywhere at all times, went on to create the physically and mentally intricate entity of man as a human being. Human, which by its very perception means fallible, prone to make errors, not perfect. In other words we wouldn't even be human if we didn't make mistakes.

Then the topper: religions proceed to describe how God is a vengeful God, a jealous God, a revengeful God. What they are describing is not a God, but rather a man. What they build is not an image of an artist which created the intricate mechanism of our reality. These petty negative connotations do not lead to an all knowing force that would build such a complex device as reality. These characteristics describe what are universally recognized as weaknesses within man, weaknesses that men strive to control.

How can religions attempt to guide men in the direction of subduing within themselves the very characteristics religions profess are inherent in the Creator Himself? Why would they do this? The only feasible answers are out of ignorance, fear, tradition, confusion, hunger for power, greed, and confusion of a rational purpose – confusion over a universal philosophy of man himself and where religion fits into the picture. Examining these characteristics leads one to the realization that these are in fact the very same characteristics that describe men. But these characteristics should not be surprising for religions are administered by men, formulated by men, perpetuated by men, and seen by men as the only significant means to keep men in check, to keep men on the "right" path.

These self serving negative behaviors of religion are not the only characteristics of religion just as they are not the only characteristics of men. Religion takes on an aura of warmth, love, concern, empathy, charity, hope, and understanding that one also finds in men. Religions, just as is the case of men, have more good in them than bad. Both religions and men have a purpose in this reality, they just have to find it in order to provide an understanding of themselves. An understanding of oneself, whether a man or an institution such as religion, is necessary before one can visualize the direction and actions one should take in this reality.

Religions, just as men, lack an understanding – a universal philosophy – of who man is, why is he here, what is his purpose as a man, as a species. Religions, like man and men, lack the understanding of where men, each of us as individuals, originated. The concepts of what happens to man after death, and how each consciousness, soul, showed up in this reality in the first place, are perplexing and are dealt with in terms of faith rather than combining what we know of faith with what we know of rationality. Religion, science, mysticism, mythology, deja vu, philosophy, all attempt to keep their own individuality rather than work together.

Religions are a guide for men. They always have been. They always will be. Religions aren't institutions. They aren't places you go on special days. They are guides to ways of life. We accept the concept of a Creator of reality. We feel it in our bones – deja vu. Looking around us we see nothing that didn't have an identifiable beginning except the reality in which we life.

We rationalize the concept that something other than man must have started the whole process. Rationalize a power of infinite power, presence, and knowledge and then proceed to make Him petty. We acknowledge that He created us as humans and then turn around and say that He will punish us because we are human and make mistakes.

The primitive attempt of developing a universal philosophy in the form of "the philosophy", says that we are extracted from God Himself and injected into this reality for a purpose. The purpose being to expand upon God's very omniscience, omnipotence, and omnipresence. This is something He cannot do Himself, as Himself, since He already is all three at once. But if this is correct, that we are a piece of God Himself, that we have a purpose in this reality, and that we will return with what we have learned, created, and experienced, then how is it that He will punish us for being exactly what He created us to be: human.

And if He would be vengeful and vindictive to us when we return, and if we are actually a part of Him and return to Him, then wouldn't punishing us be the same as punishing Himself? Are we saying that God is masochistic and sadistic in nature? That is in essence what He would be, since He would be injecting us into this reality uncertain of the absolute truth, inject us into a human form that by definition is going to make mistakes since we are in fact human, and then require that we function flawlessly under these conditions. How can men and religions move to the absurd rationality to state that God will be there to punish us for any errors we make when we return, which is in essence a form of punishing Himself.

How much more sadistic or masochistic can an entity get than to force Himself into a situation where He knows He will be unable to avoid doing wrong and then force Himself to come back once again to Himself knowing the certainty of having to face excruciating, eternal punishment. And then, of all things, inflict that very punishment upon Himself.

Some religions have a way out of this. They say, "We have a way out for you. Just believe in our religion and you will not have to suffer any punishment." Billions of other people will suffer because they don't believe, but you won't. A man living an exemplary life but not believing or consciously rejecting that very belief will go to hell and a man professing belief in these particular doctrines won't suffer even if he lives a life contrary to the teachings but repents.

Something is wrong in this logic. They trust in the words, *"Vengeance is mine; I will repay, saith the Lord."* Perhaps the words are interpreted to make what one wishes of the phrase. Perhaps the meaning isn't that the Creator isn't going to take vengeance upon returning souls but rather that we as souls need not concern ourselves with vengeance. If He isn't going to take vengeance for people harming others and if we aren't to take vengeance for people who harm others, then who is going to do it? Are people going to be able to commit all types of actions contrary to the good of their fellow souls in order to fulfill their self indulgences at the expense of other souls?

A universal philosophy would have to address this immensely crucial concept. "The philosophy" does address this concept. It does so by supporting religions, acting as their foundations, and taking them from their position of being several steps in back of mankind's philosophical and scientific development, and propelling religions back into the present so they too can once again walk hand and hand with man, science, mysticism, deja vu, and philosophy.

"The philosophy" does this by providing a rational explanation of who man is, where he came from, what his purpose is, and where he is going. So where does vengeance fit into the picture? No one wants to think that the "bad guy" is going to get away with it again. It happens too often in our present society. If God is far above the petty concept of vengeance and if we are to leave vengeance to God, then doesn't the "bad guy" have nothing to fear?

No one is going to punish the "bad guy". No one has to. He is going to do it to Himself. He is going to feel more punishment than any God or soul could wish upon Him. Remember the ripple effect? The ripple effect is not a form of God punishing a soul. It is not a matter of you being vengeful upon a soul. It just is. It is the concept that as a piece of God, each man will return to God and once again become a part of the omnipresent, omnipotent, omniscient force. As such one will be fully aware of what one has done in this reality. As such one will truly empathize in every sense of the word with what one has caused others to feel. If you have been unjustly wronged, used, abused, tormented, intimidated, scarred, or ignored by some soul, the soul contributing to the problem will know it, feel it, live it. But it won't stop there. The soul participating in the problem will also sense the repercussions of the ripple effect, in all sense of the words, in regards to negative actions you generate due to the negative actions inflicted upon you.

If it helps any, punishment will be felt and it will be swift and it will be acute. It will not, however, be initiated by God. You can breathe a sigh of relief for it will also not be your "fault". Rather, and this is the ironic part, it will be brought upon the individual by the individual himself. Souls are constantly in the process of generating their own hell.

The stress here has been upon the negative, but the same goes for the positive results. The decision one needs to make is what results do you as an individual, as a soul, want to live with into eternity? You have free will. You will reap your rewards, some "hell" and some "heaven". How much of each is in your own hands.

What does this have to do with the concept, "God's going to get you for that"? Simple; God isn't going to "get you for that". He isn't that petty, that little. He has bigger and more important things to do than that. Your fellow souls aren't going to "get you for that". Once individual souls return to becoming apart of omnipotent, omniscient, and omnipresent again, they will have enough to do sharing and experiencing their own actions and workings generated within the reality in which they just journeyed.

There are so many aspects to which this concept of "punishment" applies. Women feel guilty when raped feeling like they must have done something wrong, for they think "why else would this have happened to me?" Children feel guilty when a divorce takes place for they think, "why else would this have happened to me?" People losing a loved one, people becoming inflicted with terminal illness, spouses being abused, people losing their jobs, and on and on feel guilty when these things happen to them for they think, "why else would this have happened to me?"

We need to throw out the concept that we are being punished in life and get on with living. That does not mean to say that people should not mourn. They must mourn. It is part of being human, it's part of letting go, it's part of expressing a deep sense of loss. But people have no universal philosophy to put tragedies into perspective. A universal philosophy explaining one's purpose on earth, where one came from, and where one will be going, would greatly help religions console victims, and help victims to understand their relationship to eternity. Understand that misfortunes are not thrust upon them as punishment but rather that they just happen as a part of life. It is then up to us as individuals to decide how we will handle misfortune and tragedies.

Unfortunate events are just that – unfortunate events, not punishments. They just happen. This is an important statement for it suddenly removes the sense of guilt associated with the belief that the misfortune was brought about as a form of punishment for evil action. It removes the sense that misfortunes are bestowed upon good people and the concept that they "certainly didn't deserve it". Misfortunes and tragedies then become events in life with which we have to find a means to cope, events with which we should as fellow souls assist other souls to cope with. The concept of misfortunes being punishments for wrongdoings needs to be discarded by man.

It may have been an outstanding tool to use to control men and society in the past, but today men and society have too many problems to resolve. They do not need the burden of guilt to slow them down. Tragedies and misfortunes are difficult enough without our having to feel guilty regarding them. They are not needed to keep men in check in today's age. The concept of punishment by God may have kept all levels of men in check through fear in the past, but today that is not the case.

The concept only causes "good" people to fret and reinforces people who will do anything to get what they want at the expense of other people. It's time we start assisting the pillars of society and take the burden of "God's going to get you for that" off their back. It's time we make our children feel more at ease in their journey through our reality. It's time we build closer ties and make peace with our Creator, with other souls, with our own soul.

God is Going to Get You for That

God Doesn't Inflict Vengeance Upon Himself

"In Summary"

Vengeance – Universally Taught

Vengeance Is Used As A Tool Of Fear

God Is Us, We Are God

God Punishing Us Is God Punishing Himself

God Is Neither A Masochist Nor A Sadist

You Do Not Need To Punish Others

Misfortunes And Tragedies Are A Part Of Life, Not A Punishment

We Don't Need More Guilt

We Need To Get On With Our Lives

"We have to learn yet that all religions, under whatever name they may be called – either Hindu, Buddhist, Mohammedan, or Christian – have the same God: and he who derises any one of these derises his own God."

Vovelananda (1863 – 1902)
Indian Hindu religious leader

Chapter 31:
Christianity/Religions
♦
All Are One

Christianity is my religion. It is my niche, my comfort zone for my soul. It is where my soul has gone to find its peace as mentioned in the sections **God** and **The Ripple Effect**. This is not a section intended to convert. It is instead probably the most important section of **Part II: The Impact, Putting 'the philosophy' To the Test** since it puts "the philosophy" to its greatest test. It requires a Christian writer to explain how he can be a Christian, yet still accept and respect the teachings of others. It is a put up or shut up section for the author, since the premise of "the philosophy" is to build upon what all men already have ingrained upon their souls, their philosophies of life, and therefore it can by no means make light of their religions.

Christianity is my religious background. I do believe. I just don't believe everything exactly as the Church historically has taught. I believe in Jesus Christ. I believe He was sent. I believe He is "a **way**", not "the way." When I was young, the

Church in which I grew up believed that Christ was "the way, the truth, and the light". Now many religions are being more open and more tolerant. They are accepting other religions as another means to the same end. They recognize that the God of all significant religions is the same God, just called by a different name.

Many Christians are beginning to recognize that if Christianity is "a" way and "the" way for some, then there must be other ways. These other ways must be other religions or life beliefs by which others live. If this be the case, than the other ways must be what all of the religions past and present have in common. What they all appear to have in common is the concept of "**good**" and "**bad**". Christians are beginning to recognize the irrationality of the idea that God set up the world in such a fashion as to have 95% of all Mankind be condemned to "**eternal Hell**" as many churches profess. The whole concept of all non-Christians being condemned to eternal hell does fit "the philosophy", but it doesn't. It is an apparent paradox of "the philosophy" that is not a paradox.

It fits "the philosophy" because according to "the philosophy" all men are condemned to hell (see: **The Ripple Effect, Is It Worth It In The End, and Heaven/Hell**). It is in synch with Christianity because Christianity believes in the concept of heaven and hell.

Comparison:

Christianity

1. some men will experience hell
2. some men will go to heaven
3. all men who believe in Christ will be forgiven
4. No man shall enter the kingdom of heaven but through me"

"the philosophy" paradox

1. some men will experience hell + all others will also (ripple effect)
2. some men will go to heaven + all others will also (ripple effect)
3. all men are forgiven, but they will have to live with the knowledge, empathy, and true understanding of their actions in the "labs" of God (man being human will be truly accepted in the end and following teachings of Christ means following teachings of all great religions)
4. no man will experience "heaven" unless they follow the life pattern of Christ, which is the basic pattern of all religions

The term "religion" should be defined as the universal beliefs of man. "The philosophy" is not a religion, it is just a theoretical explanation of our purpose in life. It attempts to build upon what we as men already have. It is intended to do so without destroying, weakening, or compromising any faiths. It accepts the foundations of all religions, that our fellow men are important and we must treat them accordingly. It just adds a step. The step explaining the actual reason why all men, including ourselves, are important. It explains why intolerance of others or rejection of the value of any man's life is totally unacceptable. It explains why and when it may be more important to give up one's life for another, or for an idea. It explains why we cannot accept, through inaction, the failure of ourselves or others to respect the integrity of another man – any man. It explains why racism, elitism, social outcasting, and intolerance are not logical, acceptable, or to be tolerated.

It also gives religions and men in general an explanation and argument of why some "religions" are not religions. Satanism and certain cults are not religions and should not be recognized as such. They are not concepts universally recognized by man as subconscious thoughts, through deja vu, that have warmed the hearts and souls of men since the beginning of mankind (**The Universe, One of many labs**). They are not concepts that all men hold dear as beliefs that run so deep they seem to touch the very souls of all men. They are not concepts that men would embrace as a means to aid all men and foster the unity of mankind in its attempt to break out into its next venture, the age old yearning of man, our journey into the heavens.

The explanation of what our purpose is in life does not go against the grain of Christianity, nor does it go against the grain of any major religion. Rather it reinforces those religions and actually gives them more, not less, status in the lives of men.

The major religions of the world are meant to act as guides for men. They are teachings to show men how to interact with others, how to deal with life's problems, and how to truly accept oneself for who we ourselves are. Religions are meant to be man's shelter when he is troubled and to do this, they must feel like home to the soul, they must feel cozy to the soul, they must be the niche for that particular soul. To do this, they must be unique. They must allow some flexibility to accommodate some digression of the soul embracing it, but not so much flexibility the religion loses its own identity. They must be tolerant, loving, kind, and embracing in order to act as resting places for souls unable to find the niche that is home to them.

"The philosophy" is a theoretical, philosophical idea that precedes religion in the order of logic, for religions are the manuals of life. "The philosophy" is the reason for the manuals. Is "the philosophy" more important? By NO means! The manuals do all the work, explain all the nitty gritty, are the detailed explanation of "how to". They ARE the guidelines we go to when we are unsure of the actions to be taken. They are the resting place for our souls.

"The philosophy" just provides the reason for the manuals and gives the manuals legitimacy. "The philosophy" is simply an explanation of why. Is it the first of all steps? No! There are many more first steps to be found by man. It is just the end of the beginning. We are on an exciting, purposeful, and mind-boggling journey, and we are now at the stage of complexity requiring the input and energy of all men in a unified effort. We will need the input of every single individual in order to be successful in our journey to the far reaches of this universe. We will need the assistance of all religions, so that all men may find a resting place for their souls as they aid in this journey.

In order for all men to work together, which calls for the elimination of intolerance, we must understand the reason, the purpose, of our existence. We must know why we should maintain the integrity of our religions. We must "understand" or we will continue to sink in the eddy of intolerance and competing religions. "The philosophy" explains "why". It explains our purpose in this reality. It justifies religions even though they need no justification, for they are right. It just explains why they are right.

"The philosophy" is NOT a religion, it explains why, what the purpose of man is. It does not destroy Christianity, it reinforces it. It does not undermine religions, it legitimizes them. "The philosophy" is one step preceding religions. Religions explain how. Their answer to "why" or "what is the purpose of life" is for some to glorify God, for others to reach Nirvana etc., etc. But the question still remains "why", "what is the purpose"? Religion falls back on the concept of "faith" and "belief" when push comes to shove, and when one approaches the most basic question of "why". This is not "bad", it's just that they didn't have the reason, so they reverted to the concept "I don't know why, it just is. No, I don't know as a fact, I just have faith, I believe."

This approach was necessary in the past because no one knew "why". Nobody knows "why" still. "The philosophy", however, attempts to grapple with just that question. Using mans' past philosophical thoughts, present scientific development, creatively developed futuristic concepts proposed by others, universal religious traditional thoughts that have survived the millennia, and throwing in a dash of innovation, up pops a possible reason. The reason? Who knows? A possible reason? Yes.

"The philosophy" is an attempt at a step before religion. A universal answer to the question of "why", "what's the purpose". It may not be the reason, but it is temporarily a reason. Religions need this step to be established to legitimatize their existence and their own purpose or they will eventually be lost in today's rapid advances of technology, science, initiation of new philosophies, new age concepts, and intolerance to the age old religious response of "just because", "because you must have faith", "God is bigger than all of us", "God knows what He is doing so just listen to me" etc., etc.

Religions already are shucking their cloaks of traditions set in thousands of years of tradition. This is truly a sad event. The need to do so does not exist, in fact quite the opposite is true. The reason to do so is legitimate. Another paradox, but easily resolved through understanding the reason for man's existence.

The reason religions are shucking their traditions, is to open themselves to more tolerance of each other, which is exactly the reason for the development of "the philosophy". They believe that to gain more tolerance of each other, they need to be more like each other. They have overlooked the fact they are already alike in basic principle. They just haven't been looking at the correct basic principles. They see them in terms of Christ, the Virgin Mary, the coming of the "real" Christ, Mohammed is the "real" prophet, Buddha is mans' religious leader, etc. These are not the basic principles, they are the periphery.

Understanding "the philosophy", the purpose of man, will give religions a better grasp of what their purpose is. Through this will come tolerance of one religion for another and through tolerance will come the recognition that religions can coexist as unique entities, just as men can coexist as unique individuals. In fact, religions will begin to realize they have a responsibility to remain unique and not to become tolerant through becoming uniform, not to become tolerant through the loss of their very identities. They can perform one of their special functions by remaining unique so that the immense variety of men's souls may seek out and find a unique home in which to rest while that very soul seeks to accomplish its purpose in the **laboratory of God**.

The present trend of religions to shuck their individuality can and should be reversed. Many souls are already entering states of anxiety and turmoil from the breaking off of traditions by the church itself. Take as an example, the Catholic Church, the elimination of kneelers, removal of candles, total removal of Latin, minimizing the need of confession, etc., is the rejection of thousands of years of tradition. Modification of their meaning, maybe. Elimination of the traditions, no. Elimination of the uniqueness, the very individuality of religions themselves, is very destructive. It is the process of burning down the very home of a multitude of souls. The process of stripping a religion of its tradition is the process of stripping the religion of its uniqueness and removing just one more unique home, one more unique location, for unique sanctuary into which souls themselves may take comfort.

Religions need a preceding step. A step to answer the question, "why, what's man's and mans' purpose", in order to not lose themselves in the acceleration of man's thoughts, logic, and attack upon faith itself. Just "have faith" is rapidly becoming unacceptable to more and more people. It will not be enough of a reason to hold religion intact in the near future. If "the philosophy" does not temporarily fill this step, then we must seek another philosophy, another answer, for much of mans' future depends upon finding the answer to the age old question of "So why? What's the point of it all?" Tolerance of others, of diversified religions, of ideas, of our very selves will not be universal until we have that answer. Until the answer to the question, "Why, what's the purpose of man?" is resolved, tolerance will never become universal, regardless of how hard religions attempt to push the concept of tolerance. In fact, unless this question is answered, religions themselves will dissolve into insignificance and man will continue to swirl in the eddy of fragmentized philosophy forever.

Christianity / Religions

All Are One

"In Summary"

The Test: Christianity vs. "the philosophy"

All Religions Aren't Religions

"the philosophy" Is NOT A Religion

"the philosophy" Just Explains "Why"

"the philosophy" Legitimizes Religion

Conformity Is Truly A Sad Event For Religions And The Souls Of Men

We Must Put A Stop To The Burning Down Of The Homes Of The Soul!

The Eternal Eddy Of Fragmentized Philosophy

"The whole of history is incomprehensible without Him [Jesus]."

Ernest Renan (1823 –1892)

Chapter 32:
Jesus Christ
♦
There Is No Conflict With "the philosophy"

"The philosophy", being an explanation of the purpose of man and mankind, is intended to be a building tool for all religions. Therefore, its goal must be to reconcile the concept of Jesus Christ, Christianity, and other religions while at the same time it establishes itself as a universal initial step for all religions.

The section, **Christianity/Religions**, was written to demonstrate the reason for "the philosophy's" importance to all religions without undermining Christianity or any other religion. To the contrary, in fact, "the philosophy" strongly supports the need of a large variety of religions. It specifically calls for not only a continuation of religious traditions, but it supports a need to reestablish many of the traditions that have been erroneously eliminated. Present processes attempt to unite religions through conformity. "The philosophy" attempts to unite religions through understanding the purpose of man which in turn calls for religious tolerance and explains the very reason for the need to actually encourage a multitude of religions.

Then comes the question, how can "the philosophy" assist establishing the legitimacy of Christianity without impinging upon the turf of other religions? How can "the philosophy" allow for the expansion of religions through **missionary work** without having them infringe upon one another?

One thing at a time, starting with establishing the legitimacy of Christianity without impinging upon the turf of other religions. "The philosophy" described in Part I of this book puts forward and provides the logic for several assumptions: God is an omniscient being and needs the stimulation of creativity to prevent becoming just "a thing". In addition, "the philosophy" says, something can be made from nothing; voids were created to allow for the establishment of labs, isolated from the omniscient; voids were created to generate new knowledge; man has a soul that is actually a part of God; man must have free will; and lastly, that all this was established for a purpose of which man is a part.

Quite a project! And those three words, omniscience, omnipresence, omnipotence, are the very reason for the concept of Christ and yet provides for the legitimacy of other religions without conflict and thus introduces the beginning of universal tolerance with the logic to back it up. Providing the rationality and the logic for universal tolerance provides the foundation for the acceptance of worldwide tolerance and establishes its permanency.

Assume that all the premises of "the philosophy" are correct, or crudely so, then the effort to create the universe and its many labs of creativity would have been a very complex and intricate project. The effort involved, the desire for the product it could produce, and the intense hope of seeing a personal creation succeed, would be enough to make any omnipotent, omniscient, omnipresent being do whatever it could to keep its creation from self destruction. It would be imperative, however, to do so without actually, in the process, destroying the creation or the purpose of the creation itself.

Looking at mans' history, it would be said by many that man, two thousand years ago, was on a very long-term violent and self-destructive path. A man's life was worth little in the regions of the west where much change was taking place in terms of mans' accumulation of knowledge and projected influence on earth's future history. The path was turning towards an acceleration of the demeaning of an individual's life. Violence, and the decline of "moral" philosophical behavioral guidelines, were becoming unbearable. History is a massive object to develop and it takes massive quantities of time and energy to shift its momentum, its direction. The shift has to begin somewhere, however, in order to begin.

"The philosophy" asserts that all souls are a piece of God and go back to God. "The philosophy" also asserts God cannot enter the voids without jeopardizing the very purpose of the voids in the first place, the creative development of the "new" and the "unknown" for the Omniscient. God would be aware of what was taking place in the voids it created since all souls would be continually returning to their source, God.

Through this manner, God would be aware of the direction in which men were headed. This could have been threatening enough to God's creation that He might have been very well looking for a means by which He could thwart this development. A means to provide the gentle but massive initial thrust needed to correct the trajectory of mankind and thus begin the slow steady correction in the path of mans' long future development.

How simple a technique to just interject a soul, as always, but this time it would be a soul that had not only free will as other souls had, but also was given an inner need to fulfill a predestined purpose. It would be a soul that also had just a little more understanding of the purpose of man and, in particular, his own purpose on earth. A man who was God, as we all are, but who sensed his connection with God better than the rest of us do. A man who, it might be argued, through his awareness and his soul being released with free will, yet with a fuller understanding of its specifically predestined purpose, might actually be a little closer to God and thus be more God on this earth than the rest of us.

His purpose, to turn the tide of mans' outlook away from violence and devaluation of the individual back towards the concepts of tolerance and recognition of the value of each individual, for each individual houses a soul and each soul has a purpose. A purpose essential to God Himself. A purpose essential to each and every soul itself.

Christ. God Himself? Yes. Sent by God? Yes. Sent by God for a reason? Yes. Sent to reestablish man's tie to God, to reestablish man's tie to other men? Yes. Sent to reestablish that man must follow the teachings of God? Yes.

Christ. Sent to set up his own kingdom of religious dominance? No. Sent to provide a clear understanding of man's purpose? No. Sent to establish that no man is acceptable in the eyes of the Creator unless he embraces the individual of Christ Himself? No.

Thus Christianity and other religions have the same purpose, the same basic beliefs, the same goals. They just use different peripherals to get there. Religions are compatible. They can be tolerant to each other without committing self destruction. They may and should retain their uniqueness in order to provide the multitude of unique homes for the vast number of unique souls. Religions are resting places, homes, for the weary traveler, the soul itself.

Jesus Christ / "the philosophy"
There Is No Conflict

"In Summary"

Jesus Was God

Jesus Was Sent By God

Through Jesus Men Will Be Saved

God Has A Vested Interest In His Creation

Religions Are Compatible

Tolerance Applies To Religions

Unique Souls Require Unique Resting Places

Religions Are Resting Places For The Soul

"Our destiny exercises its influence over us even when, as yet, we have not learned its nature: it is our future that lays down the law of our today."

Friedrich Wilhelm Nietzsche
Human, All Too Human, 1878

In Summary
♦
*History Is Not Meant For The Present
Past Reflections Are Meant To Guide One Into The Future*

There are three parts to a person's life: the past, the present, and the future. The shortest of these is the present for it is but a fleeting point in time. Everything we remember is already in the past and everything we will experience is in the future. What is happening now has already happened. In other words the present is as small an increment of time as the geometric concept of the size of a point is of a line. One, therefore, should not study history to change the present, for the present is already the past. One should study the past so one can determine how to change the future.

It is often said by historians that one should study history to avoid repeating the past. This concept is significantly different than studying history so one can determine how to change the future.

We are at a new point in time. We are on the threshold of moving into the stars. We are on the threshold of understanding just who we are and what our purpose in this reality is. Man is teetering on the edge of a new age. A new age glistening with the tolerance for all souls, with the admiration of uniqueness of institutions and individual journeys of souls, with a true sense of an understanding of our connection to the souls of all men, to God Himself.

A change has to take place within our minds, within our society, before we can step into the new age. We have to do something that has never been done before. We have to develop a universal philosophy that embraces all men and respects the comfort level of their souls. A philosophy that reinforces past traditions and encourages uniqueness and individuality. A philosophy that binds men together in a common cause. A philosophy that pictures the brotherhood of souls not as a hope or a goal, but as a fact, an absolute.

The development of such a philosophy will lead us to look at the past in an entirely different manner. It will lead us to examine the past not with the hope of avoiding repeating it, for this is an examination filled with depression and despair. This type of approach shows nothing but the continual repetition of man repeating history itself. This type of approach has been the focus of mans' study of the past since the beginning of man.

We have to take an upbeat, positive, and optimistic approach when we study the past or we are going to inevitably repeat out past mistakes. We cannot enter a new age without changing our past behavior. History, the past, therefore has to be examined not for the purpose of preventing the repeat of our past, but rather for the purpose of changing our future, for improving our future, for providing an environment that will allow souls to journey in freedom, safety, cleanliness, and in an aura of excitement, security, delight, acceptance, and awe.

We have to provide homes for the souls: religion. We have to build support for the souls. We have to establish acceptance of all souls. We have to . . . We have to . . . We have to . . . So much to do, so little time. So much to do, so few to do it. All of our energies need to be expended in working to expand the very essence of the all-powerful, all-knowing, all-present force that sent us here. We must expend our energies for all of us, for He is Us, and We are He.

That means we need to look at the past and examine how our intolerances toward others have lead to trauma of individual souls within society. We must reexamine our past actions and ask, "Has our past behavior towards homosexuals, drug addicts, emotionally crippled, physically crippled, our environment in which other souls will travel, people professing other religious beliefs than ours, the sick, the old, the young, and even ourselves, been beneficial for the journey of these very souls, our soul?"

If the answer is no, then we must not go on with the thought in mind that we do not want to repeat it, but rather with the conviction that we must change it and recognizing the fact that we now have a mission to address. We must then expend part of our social resources to doing just that. This approach provides a purpose, an ideal for people to reach out to and strive to attain. This approach provides a purpose in people's lives, their journey through this reality. It provides hope.

There are so many needs for the future. There are so many things in the past we need to change for the future that everyone is needed in the effort. We need people to examine what should be and what shouldn't be changed. People need to be organizing the process of putting the changes in place. Human energy needs to be expended in making the changes. The process of continual revision, modification, and fine tuning will take countless people. The actual dismantling of old ideas, institutions, and detriments in our environment that hamper the journey of souls is mind-boggling in scope. We need every soul available to join in the effort.

Then comes the work needed to not just provide the extra effort to get mankind into the new age, but the extra effort needed to actually thrust us into the heavens themselves. Surely we do not want to enter the realm of other intellectual life forms in a whimper. Surely we want to enter the realm of the heavens as a proud, united, cohesive, colorful, confident entity. Surely we want to enter the realms of the heavens with the emotions of excitement, anticipation, understanding, tolerance, and respect exuding from each and every one of us. Surely we want the entrance of our species into the wonders of space, a new species entrance, to be one of magnificence and significance.

Let's not make this step, a step into a new stage of our journey, one that follows our past traditions. Let's not make it one encompassing intolerance, friction, fighting, bickering, greed, self indulgence, and violence. The way to prevent this is to take a more global look at our past spheres of influence. The spheres of knowledge, religion, philosophy, mysticism, deja vu, mythology must be in harmony with each other. That will take an understanding on the part of each sphere of influence as to its importance in the journey of man. A recognition that in fact they do not need to continue their patterns of competition between themselves for man's loyalty.

They need to instead recognize the importance and necessity each has in regard to man's journey. They need to recognize that they are not the item of importance to be served here but rather that they are here as a tool for man. It is man that is of importance here. It also needs to be noted that it is not the machine that man occupies that is of importance, for that also is but a tool; rather it is the soul itself, for the soul is actually God and We are He.

To make this transition in the ranking of importance of man and institutions will take dramatic change in how we view history. It will mean we will need to look at the past with the intent to change the future. It will mean we will need to use all our resources and begin to combine the knowledge, experience, beliefs, and perceptions of religion, math, science, mysticism, mythology, deja vu, and philosophy and begin to build a universal philosophy that encompasses all men and all institutions.

It is truly an exciting time. Being able to live in a time when man, for the first time in history, is on the edge of literally stepping into the heavens, is breathtaking. If we make it this time, if we do not falter, no other generation but ours will be able to say they were at the threshold of the heavens and stepped into the sea of the stars. No other generation will be able to lay claim to having propelled man from a terrestrial being to a traveler amongst the stars. No other souls will be able to visualize themselves having journeyed during the infancy of mans' physically exploring the heavens himself, the dream of man since his very beginning.

Are we there yet? No, and it may not come about. History has never produced a civilization that has worked for the good of all men, one that does not have the self interest of participating factions large and small involved. This may not be the point in time where man will gain a significant foothold into the heavens. That would not be the end of reality and if history repeats itself, it won't be the end of mankind. The collapse would be unfortunate, however, for it would mean another setback for mankind. It would mean another setback in the recognition of the importance of each individual soul. It would once again postpone the elevation of the individual soul to its rightful place, to the recognition that each soul is a piece of God and has a purpose.

It is very possible that we will not succeed at our quest to reach the heavens at this point in our history. Not much of significance has changed in terms of the outlook we have regarding each other and who we are and what our purpose is. It is difficult to determine direction when one does not know where he is headed, what his purpose is in taking a particular action. Having just a sense of direction is different than having a light shining on the path. Having no purpose and having a purpose is like night and day while journeying down a path. At night one often stumbles over pits and rocks on the path, not to speak of the countless number of times one wanders off the path in the dark. Once off the path, it sometimes takes a good deal of time, effort, and misfortune before finding one's way back.

Sometimes a little assistance is needed to find one's way back to the path when in the dark. But add light and the journey becomes entirely different. You still stray from time to time. You still stumble over big feet, lack of concentration, and adversities, but not to the same degree. So we need a light. Somehow we need to find the switch to turn on that light. We should have the resources we need to find that switch or we wouldn't be at the brink of making the jump into the heavens.

The switch is here, we just have to know what we are looking for, and since we have never been to this point in our journey before, we may not even realize that we need to look for it. A switch, something that mankind has never had, something he has always attempted to find without knowing what it actually is. Something that all areas of mans' endeavors, religion, math, science, mysticism, mythology, deja vu, and philosophy, have striven to find.

And what is it they have all universally searched for? It appears to be an understanding of who man is, what his purpose is, where he came from before this reality, where he will be going after this reality, and what will happen to him there. In other words, man has since the beginning of time attempted to find a universal philosophy that encompasses all men, encompasses all souls, be they of men or others. A philosophy that will finally answer the question, "Who am I, and what is my purpose in reality?"

"The philosophy" may not be the answer, but maybe it will help people find the answer. A missing piece of our consciousness that has kept us in the dark so long. We need to find the switch that will lighten up the path of our journey through reality on a quest to benefit God Himself and to benefit ourselves.

The place to look: the past. The place it will take us: the future.

"In Summary"

The Present Is But A Fleeting Moment In Time

Study History To Change The Future

A Universal Philosophy Would Cause Change

So Much To Do, So Little Time

Intolerance Has Lead To Trauma

Revision, Modification, Fine Tuning

Stepping Into The Heavens

Man, Souls, Over Institutions

We Are Missing Something

The Place To Look: The Past

The Place It Will Take Us: The Future

In Conclusion

♦

"Facts which at first seem improbable will, even on scant explanation, drop the cloak which has hidden them and stand forth in naked and simple beauty."

Galilo Galilei (1564 – 1642)

The Book In Summary
♦
Two Statements/Nine Words

Two statements, nine words tell it all; but it takes seventy thousand words, over three hundred pages, and forty sections to explain the two ideas.

Seventeen thousand words paint the picture of "**the philosophy**" that answers mans' two age old questions: "Who am I?" and "What is my purpose in life?"

Fifty-three thousand words paint the picture of **the impact** of "the philosophy".

Thirty chapters are needed to simplify the understanding and compartmentalize the two concepts for the human brain to better understand.

That's it – two ideas and seventy thousand words to begin to lend the two ideas credence.

Read, enjoy, scoff, fume, ridicule, question, and immerse yourself. These are ideas painted on the canvas of the heavens, with the color of the written word and the strokes of creativity.

These ideas are painted with the purpose to draw you into the painting itself, with the hope that you will emerge a changed person. A person no longer living in a black and white existence, but a person living in a rainbow of colors and in awe of each and every one of them.

Ah, simplicity, the beauty of the universe itself.

Go in peace.

"In Summary"

Man Is God

You, I, We Have A Purpose

A Special Page Of Thanks
For all those listed here, Know you have all made a special contribution towards this book,
You have all touched, in a special way, another soul – mine.

Nancy, my wife – for her support, encouragement, honest criticism, patience, and love.

Ralph, my brother – for his awakening me to the fact that I could write this book. I just had to start.

Tim, my brother – for our midnight discussions and for his reading, honest criticism, and suggestions.

Deb, my twin – for her close companionship and support, which only twins can understand.

Hazel Proctor and Don Proctor – for their patience and unique services as publishers of my endeavor.

Terry Cunningham – for her initial encouragement, readings, editing, and suggestions.

Dorothy Chomicz – for encouraging me and providing me with the time off work to finish this book.

Dr. Weinbrenner – for his unusual professional generosity of time, compassion, and assistance that changed my life, which in turn allowed me to initiate my dream of writing this book.

Cindy Bond and Evelene Kenny – for doing such a great job working my business that I could take the time required to develop my book.

Chris, my oldest son – for his helping me understand that there is nothing more important in a soul's journey than one's influence upon other souls, brothers all in this reality's journey.

Danielle, my only daughter – for her demonstrating the concept that you need to take hold of life and control it rather than letting life push you around.

Scott, my youngest son – for his discussions with me regarding life, his unusual insights into "the philosophy", and his many contributions of ideas.

My Mother – for being what the word "Mother" personifies to me.

My Father – for his many talks and speculations.

And to all the rest of you out there that have touched my life – a special thanks.

Peace to each and every one of you.

"Math is Truly a Recreational Endeavor."
Mr. Shepard

Math Can Be Fun and Exciting

Addendum
To My Students:
Past, Present, And Yet To Come

What can I say? Thank you all. For nearly thirty years, you have been coming to me and for nearly thirty years I've enjoyed your company immensely. You have all been very stimulating, invigorating, and delightful to know. Each and every one of you has touched me in your own way, changed my outlook on life in some manner, and assisted me through my journey in life. This book was not only written for my own biological children, it was written for you.

Many are the hours that we have mingled together discussing puzzles of the universe. I have watched you grow and have found such delight in your progress that I don't know how anyone could not love being a teacher, a mentor of souls.

It is a task made for kings. I have been in the same district, the same building, teaching the same subject areas for all that time. Often I have been asked, "How can you stand working in the same place teaching the same subject all that time?"

How ludicrous a question. My journey has not had to be one of distance. Quite the contrary, for as fast as I would work, the more there would seem to be to do. It is not the miles one journeys that is of importance, rather it is the journey itself that is. Your constant entering and exiting my classroom has never stopped. I have had more than 4,000 of you come through my classroom and each and every one of you was unique. How could this type of experience be boring or drudgery? How could this task ever be finished?

There has always been so much to do, so many of you with which to interact that the task was never completed. Think of it – 4,000 growing souls to mentor. That represents over 800,000 hours of indulging in a creative art, the art of molding the future. What an occupation!

Don't be afraid to be unique. Uniqueness is the strength of our souls. Don't be afraid to work together, man is an example where the whole is actually greater than the sum of its parts, for the parts keep expanding the whole.

Part of being unique means that all of you need to find your own niche in this reality. It isn't always easy and often we may wonder if we have found it or if we should continue to look. Keep in mind not everyone is intended to do the same things or experience the same events. We are meant to journey on different paths in reality. There is much to do. My journey, your journey, have immense significance when combined with the whole.

Many are the hours we have, together, examined the concept of respecting others. Many are the hours you have directly participated in these discourses regarding tolerance. Sometimes you were the injured party, sometimes you were the perpetrator. Many more were the times you have sat in class and observed as the discourses took place around you, learning through the experiences of others. Your journey in life is like that, for you learn and experience through others as well as yourself. This is an important point, for it means you influence reality not only through your direct actions but just as importantly, through the model you generate for others as they observe how you journey through life.

Often as we have discussed math and science, you have broached the subject of their importance to you in life. During many of these times, granted not as many as you would have liked, we have dropped what we were doing and talked about the universe and about its marvelous perplexities, complexities, and secrets. All of this tied into math, the language of science, the universal language of our reality.

The experience of having been able to walk with you for a short time, as you journeyed through reality, has been wonderful. I have always wanted to find a way to tell each and every one of you that. I know when I see many of you, I may not remember your names. You change so quickly during your pre and early teen years, which does nothing but compound my faulty circuit for name recall. But remembering your name is not the important thing here. The effect you have on others and the effect they have had on you is what is important. You need to know that all of you have touched and helped to mold my very essence. You need to know that my soul feels at peace and full, due in large part to you and the enjoyment I found in our contacts. Thank you for that.

My thanks go out to all of you. The key word here is "all". Life is a learning experience. It is not always going to be positive in nature. Those of you that needed discipline, don't look at it as a "bad" situation, a negative situation. I have enjoyed you at these times as much as in the exciting positive situations. Both were learning and growth experiences not only for you, but for me.

Many are the lessons you, through your misbehavior, have taught me so that I could move on to the next student and improve my interactions with them. Many are the experiences you have had to endure in your lives that have melted my heart and forced me to grow in compassion for the new students that were to come to me.

Take heart, all you young souls, yours is a growing time, a time when society nurtures you, models for you, and mentors you. Remember you, as is the caase with the rest of us, control your own actions. You, too, are responsible for what you do. Learn. Your soul, too, has a journey to take. If your present journey is not to your liking, know that soon you will be in complete control of your journey and you can, if you wish, put your present unpleasantries behind you.

This book was partially a by-product of you and your interactions with me. Your souls touching mine have helped to mold me and direct my thoughts. The concept of a universal philosophy is a product of the question "Why?", and we all know how many times you have asked me that question. Many are the times we have sat together and wondered over the universe, man, and philosophy.

I have told yoy many times that "math is a recreational endeavor." This book has been the outcome of simplistic mathematics intended for your enjoyment and contemplation, intended for all souls.

Don't be afraid to explore. Don't be afraid to roll back the shadows of the void of our reality. Keep yourself as healthy as you can, for your journey is long and your journey is important to all of us. Keep yourself alert, for no matter where you are, there are new opportunities for learning. Keep your mind open, for a closed mind misses out on many exciting concepts. Keep your mind healthy, for it is the most important tool you have in your journey in this reality.

For those of my students that have already established themselves as pillars in our society, remain strong even when the swirling waters of doubt continually try to pull you down. You are the support beams holding up the roof over our civilization. You are what prevents the collapse of our progress as men. Without you, the roof will collapse, civilization will be set back, and men will have to start rebuilding again.

Don't ever be afraid to ask, "Why?" It is the question that will change humankind and you are going to be the ones to ask it.

I wish you well on your journey and know that I have found great satisfaction in being able to be a part of it.

SUGGESTED READING LIST

Andromeda Strain, Michael Crichton, 1969, Knopf.
Atlas Shrugged, Ayn Rand,, 1957, Random House.
Book of Virtues: Treasury of the World's Great Moral Stories, William Bennett, 1993, Simon & Schuster.
The Bible
Brief History in Time, Steven Hawking, 1988, Bantam.
The Celestine Prophecy, James Redfield, 1994, Warner.
Chariots of the Gods, Erich Von Daniken, 1984, Berkley.
Chicken Soup for the Soul, Volumes I and II, Jack Canfield, 1993, Health Communications.
Chronolgy of the World, Isaac Asimov [out of print].
Distant Secrets: Unravelling the Mysteries of our Ancient Past, Ronald Schiller, 1989, Carol Publishing Group.
Exodus, Leon Uris, 1983, Bantam.
The Hobbitt, J.R.R. Tolkien, originally 1938, 1986, Ballantine.
Jonathan Livingston Seagull, Richard Bach, 1970, Avon.
Jungle, Upton Sinclair, 1965, Airmont.
Mere Christianity, C.S. Lewis, 1952, MacMillan.
Mutant Message Downunder, Marlo Morgan, 1991, Harper.
One Two Three Infinity, Isaac Asimov [out of print].
Parallell Myths, J.F. Bierlein, 1994, Ballantine.
Perelandra, Out of the Silent Planet, Hideous Strength, C.S. Lewis 1976, Amereon Ltd., 1980, MacMillan.
Red Storm Rising, Tom Clancy, 1987, Berkley
Screwtape Letters, C.S. Lewis, 1995, Bantam [reprint].
Trilogy: The Foundation, Isaac Asimov [out of print].
Where the Red Fern Grows, Wilson Rawls, 1984, Bantam.
Where the Sidewalk Ends, Shel Silverstein, 1974, Harper Collins.
Wisdom of the West, Bertrand Russell, 1989, Random.
Your God is Too Small, Norman Vincent Peale, J.B. Phillips, 1964, MacMillan.

ABOUT THE AUTHOR

Daniel Shepard was born in Victoria, Texas in 1945, and spent his childhood in Zeeland, Michigan. Shepard earned a B.S. Degree from the University of Michigan and a Master's Degree in Physical Science from Eastern Michigan University. He currently teaches school in Livonia, Michigan.

Shepard has been happily married to his soul mate, Nancy, for 25 years, and has three children. His main hope: to see mankind find a fundamental in life that would give strength to man's purpose and lead him to a true tolerance, understanding, and respect for himself and his fellow man.